MAINE WOMEN PIONEERS III

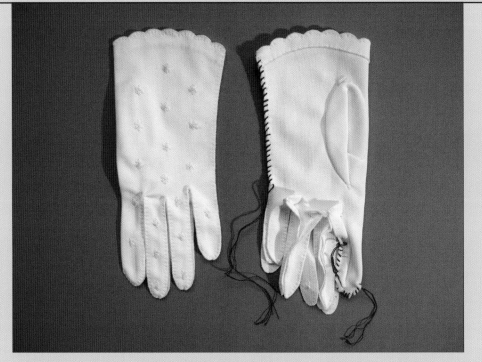

Allison Cooke Brown, *Glove (#10)*, 2012, cotton gloves and thread, 8" x 3.5" (each).

MAINE WOMEN PIONEERS III

VANGUARD
October 12–December 16, 2012

•

HOMAGE
January 2–March 3, 2013

•

WORLDVIEW
March 12–May 12, 2013

•

DIRIGO
May 22–July 21, 2013

• • •

CURATORS
Gael May McKibben
Andres Azucena Verzosa
Anne Broderick Zill

• • •

UNIVERSITY OF NEW ENGLAND ART GALLERY
IN ASSOCIATION WITH THE
CENTER FOR ETHICS IN ACTION

University of New England
716 Stevens Avenue
Portland, Maine 04103
www.une.edu/artgallery

Published on the occasion of the
Maine Women Pioneers III Exhibition
University of New England Art Gallery
Portland, Maine, October 12, 2012 through July 21, 2013.

CATALOGUE DESIGN:
Harrah Lord, Yellow House Studio
Rockport, Maine 04856, www.yellowhousestudio.info

FRONT COVER: Maggie Foskett, *Bits and Pieces*, 2007, cliché verre, 19.75" x 15.75"
BACK COVER: Arla Patch, *Please Abide with Me*, 2007, polymer clay, 29" x 25"
FRONTISPIECE: *UNE Art Gallery,* Courtesy of the University of New England Art Gallery

ISBN: 978-1-4675-5970-6
Library of Congress Control Number: 2013930777

Major funding for this catalogue publication and its companion exhibitions has been
provided by a lead grant from the Quimby Family Foundation as well as additional grants
from the Robert and Dorothy Goldberg Charitable Foundation and the Warren Memorial
Foundation. In addition, significant contributions have been received
from Albert and Judy Ellis Glickman, Barbara Goodbody, Alison Hildreth,
Kate Cheney Chappell, S. Donald Sussman, Eliot and Melanie Cutler,
Norma Marin, Susan Groce, Alice Spencer, and Rose Marasco.

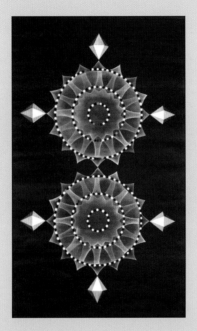

*Dedicated to
all Maine women in
the visual arts.*

• • •

To the artists of yesterday, today and tomorrow.
May your spirit forever be free.

JOHN WHITNEY PAYSON

...

CONTENTS

from the DIRECTOR

*M*aine Women Pioneers III has been ten years in the making. Many people have given their advice, insights, reflections and especially their friendship in a state-wide collaboration that has resulted in this four-part, ten-month long exhibition. I am ever grateful to the University of New England (UNE) for the opportunity to direct its Art Gallery, and to the Center for Ethics in Action for its fiscal sponsorship of the catalogue.

Funding for this exhibition, educational programs and catalogue publication has been provided by a major lead grant from the Quimby Family Foundation as well as additional grants from the Robert and Dorothy Goldberg Charitable Foundation and the Warren Memorial Foundation. In addition, significant contributions have been received from Albert and Judy Ellis Glickman, Barbara Goodbody, Alison Hildreth, Kate Cheney Chappell, S. Donald Sussman, Eliot and Melanie Cutler, Norma Marin, Susan Groce, Alice Spencer and Rose Marasco.

I thank all who helped comb the universe of Maine women artists and contributed in many other ways as well: Debra V. Barry, Bruce Brown, Annette Elowitch, June Fitzpatrick, Heather Frederick, Rosemary Frick, Peggy Golden, Mary Harding, June LaCombe, Carl Little, Suzette McAvoy, Caren-Marie Michel,

Elizabeth Moss, Leonard and Merle Nelson, Dorothy Schwartz, Katherine Watson and Margaret Yatsevitch.

Each essayist has added verbal depth, breadth, and a national view to this catalogue's content. Designer Harrah Lord is an immensely talented ally whose steady hand has guided the entire catalogue effort.

Thanks also to UNE's Dorothy Royle and Jeannine Owens as well as Yale University Art Gallery's David Whaples who have lent their individual expertise, and to UNE Gallery staff Carolyn Heasly and Ilana Welch. The exhibitions have been stunningly designed and installed with consummate skill by Kevin Callahan. Finally, I am hugely indebted to my dear friends and curator colleagues, Gael May McKibben and Andres Azucena Verzosa, who have made this whole enterprise the best experience of a lifetime.

—Anne Broderick Zill

It was social and art historian William David Barry whose idea it was, tickling him over a number of years, to take a look at Maine's women artists in the 19th century. We explored together, doing research and traveling the state to find the artists' work subsequently included in the 1981 exhibition, *Women Pioneers in Maine Art.* It seemed perfectly natural to follow that with a look at women artists of the first part of the 20th century—to see what the opportunities and changes were. And now, into the late second and early third century beyond the first identification of some of the "pioneers," what an explosion, what a massive change, what a new world it is for Maine's women artists!

Granted, there have been equal changes in societal mores, in industrial development, in technology. The women in this exhibition have benefitted from the changes, have been freed to grow, to explore, to push boundaries, to experiment with new mediums, to show their work near and far, to participate in dialogues with other artists, critics, donors, collectors, to contribute to the greater global art world.

To quote Dahlov Ipcar, "Artists should create new visions not just repeat reality." And these artists in *Maine Women Pioneers III,* as well as the many others not represented here, have been doing just that.

To have been a part of this, to have worked again with scholar Joan Uraneck and with Anne Zill and Andy Verzosa, has been a privilege and honor.

•

Gael May McKibben was Assistant Director of the Joan Whitney Payson Gallery of Art during its lifetime, 1977 until 1991. During one of the periods as Acting Director, she co-curated the first Maine Women Pioneers exhibition with William David Barry and then, two years later, the second, *Maine Women Pioneers: 1900–1945.* When the Gallery closed and its permanent collection moved to the Portland Museum of Art, she joined its registrar's office and was briefly Acting Registrar. Later she served as Executive Director of the Maine Crafts Association, bridging and helping to close the distinction between fine art and fine crafts.

• • •

In 1998, I discovered a cache of vintage watercolors by Alice Harmon Shaw (1913–1994) in an antique store on Portland's waterfront. A few years later, I opened Aucocisco Galleries, with *Bright Visions of Place,* a show of that artist's very same works. As reference material of her mother's previous shows, her daughter had given me catalogues from the first Maine Women Pioneer exhibitions mounted in 1981 and in 1984 at what was affectionately called "the little jewel box," the Joan Whitney Payson Gallery of Art at Westbrook College.

What a find those catalogues were! The pioneer aesthetic captured my attention in an historical sense but, more importantly, in a contemporary sense because of its timeliness, discovery, and inherent challenge—I was intrigued. Original MWP curator and historian William David Barry writes, "Each generation, in fact, has to face shifting attitudes, circumstances, and possibilities, which are fundamentally different from those, which existed before. If one accepts this view of dynamic change, it becomes proper and necessary to acknowledge that each era produces its own pioneers." And, "By acknowledging that their ground-breaking visions were also aesthetically fine, we award them pioneering status on the grounds of quality, rather than simply being there first."

Fortified with this framework I was eager to see what a Maine Women Pioneers exhibit might look like today. So inspired, I contacted my colleague Anne Zill at the University of New England Art Gallery to discuss the likelihood of mounting a new exhibition. Anne and I are known quantities to one another having collaborated together on *Prelude to an Apocalypse* at the Gallery in 2002, one year after the 9/11 catastrophes. Thus the seed was planted; but it took several years for the proposal of mounting a third installment of MWP to germinate and sprout. The stars aligned in the fall of 2009.

That is when Gael May McKibben joined us. She was one of the original curators who had worked along with William David Barry on the two earlier MWP shows.

But this was going to be a challenge.... The artists we hoped to work with were very much alive, and there were so many of them! Despite the challenges, the three of us began the curatorial process in earnest by soliciting input and advice from scores of respected members of the visual arts community. We compiled lists of names. We talked about the attributes and merits of them all. Process. Patterns and similarities and differences and distinctions were apparent. Clusters formed. Thus the basis of our four-part exhibition began to emerge as a logical outcome. The other decision, apart from which artists would be included in MWP III, became the context in which they would be presented. We decided to engage writers to assist in pulling together the context that would connect these women artists to contemporary issues and concerns. Our conversations centered primarily on how we wanted to show these women as pioneers and why.

I am grateful to have played a role in getting MWP III off the ground, and I am proud to have worked with my fellow co-curators in such a thoughtful and innovative collaboration. MWP III just could not have happened without the help of many but certainly not without my colleagues Anne and Gael.

In closing, I would like to personally

dedicate MWP III to two Maine women very close to my heart, Helen Friend Langlais and Lucille Minqueau Webb, who were not artists themselves but were champions of art and are an inspiration to me everyday.

•

Andres A. Verzosa is deeply committed to Maine's arts and cultural life. In 2000, he established Aucocisco Galleries and founded Portland's First Friday Art Walk. He serves on the boards of the Maine College of Art, the Maine Irish Heritage Center, the Ogunquit Museum of American Art, and the Tides Institute & Museum of Art. Most recently he served on the board of the Quimby Family Foundation and was former president of the Portland Arts & Cultural Alliance. He is co-editor of Maine Art New a book on contemporary art in Maine, scheduled for publication 2013.

• • •

My commitment to *Maine Women Pioneers III*, when Andy Verzosa first mentioned it a decade ago, was immediate. Yes! I wanted to create an exhibition to celebrate Maine women artists alive and working today who have so much to teach us, and for whom the word "pioneer" still fits. I embraced the term used by Guggenheim Museum Director James Johnson Sweeney in the 1950s—"tastebreakers"—who "break open and enlarge our artistic frontiers."

Working with two other curators meant that a lot of give and take was required. We agreed no survey show would be possible. Not only would the "pioneer" designation lose currency but the UNE Gallery simply would not be big enough. We had to be both rigorous and provocative. Our values, our vision and our scholarship had to stand the test of time so that 100 years from now the MWP III catalogue would remain a timeless testament to 51 Maine women artist innovators working in the early 21st century.

Over a period of many months in a series of long dinners and full afternoons we hammered out our goals and strategies. Once we agreed on the exhibition's structural architecture, we could sift the artists into different shadings of art categories that "pushed the artistic envelope." The logic of Vanguard, Homage, Worldview and Dirigo—a four-part exhibition—began to emerge.

Other Pioneer shows in the future? Yes! But let us revel in this valuable exhibition and accompanying catalogue now!

•

Anne Broderick Zill is a graduate of Barnard College with a MA from American University. She is a founder of the Women's Campaign Fund. A longtime program associate of the Stewart Mott Foundation, she has been the director of the UNE Art Gallery for 15 years. She has mounted two exhibitions of global women's art at the United Nations, and in 2012 an exhibition of women's photographs at UNESCO.

REVISITING LINDA NOCHLIN'S QUERY

Joan P. Uraneck

*"Even a simple question like 'Why have there been no great women artists?' can,
if answered adequately . . . challenge the assumption that the traditional divisions of intellectual
inquiry are still adequate to deal with the meaningful questions of our time . . ."*

LINDA NOCHLIN
"WHY HAVE THERE BEEN NO GREAT WOMEN ARTISTS?"
Art News, January 1971

MAINE WOMEN PIONEERS III is the third exhibition focused on women artists in Maine that the University of New England Art Gallery has mounted over the past thirty years. The first (1981) featured women artists working in the nineteenth century. The second (1985) showcased Maine women artists working between 1900 and 1945. These exhibitions researched and brought to light the invisible and marginalized women artists working in these times. *Maine Women Pioneers III* deals with women artists working in the period from 1945 to the present. What is very apparent in MWP III is that women artists are alive and well and actively participating not only in Maine's art world but beyond. They are exhibiting their work in galleries and museums; they are receiving grants and fellowships; they are teachers in colleges and universities; and they are leaders in the contemporary art scene in Maine. The degree of their presence in comparison to their absence in the nineteenth and early twentieth century is remarkable. Clearly, significant changes have occurred in the place and role of women artists in the contemporary art world. One can't help but wonder, what brought about these changes? In looking back over the period since 1945, there is no question that the trigger that is responsible for this change is the feminist movement of the sixties and seventies. It has indeed caused a major social and cultural revolution and it is very apparent in MWP III.

Much has happened since 1945, both artistically and socially: a long line of "isms" (Abstract Expressionism, Pop Art,

Minimalism, Postmodern, etc.) and two major social movements, the civil rights movement of the 1950s and the feminist movement also known as the Women's Movement, Women's Liberation or Women's Lib of the 1960s and 1970s. Both the civil rights movement and the feminist movements cried out for equal rights and opportunities and for the end of discrimination. Both have caused upheavals that have changed the world. So, are things different? You bet, and especially for women artists, and nowhere is that more evident than in *Maine Women Pioneers III*.

Feminism broke into the art world through Linda Nochlin's incredible essay "Why Have There Been No Great Female Artists?" Published in *Art News* in 1971, it challenged the patriarchal art world and shook it to its roots. Nochlin claimed that women's failure to have attained greatness lay "not in our stars, our hormones, our menstrual cycles or our empty internal spaces" but in our institutions. Her answer to her own question was that society was at fault. It was the lack of opportunities for education and training in the arts that historically had kept women "out of the picture." It was also the lack of opportunities to be seen and known, to have patrons, to be included in exhibitions and to be written about, and of course, the longstanding societal expectations for women to be wives and mothers that hindered the emergence of women artists.

Clearly things have changed on this front. Unlike their predecessors in MWP I and II, MWP III artists have had access to training and education. While some are self-taught, most are professionally trained in art schools, colleges and universities. Many hold not only BFA but also MFA degrees and from well known institutions such as the University of Pennsylvania, Columbia, SUNY, N.Y., Bard, Washington University and many others. The advantages of this kind of training are not just that women are getting the kind of technical training needed to be productive and successful but also the credentials to participate in the professional world.

Many of the exhibitors hold teaching positions in colleges and universities. Just to name a few, Lois Dodd taught for 25 years at Brooklyn College of Art, Denise Froehlick teaches at Bates, Meggan Gould is Assistant Professor of Art at Bowdoin, Barbara Sullivan at the University of Maine at Farmington, Yvonne Jacquette at Moore College of Art, the University of Pennsylvania and Parsons.

Lois Dodd, *Bee Approaching Touch Me Nots*

Rose Marasco has taught at the University of Southern Maine for almost thirty years. Melita Westerland has taught at the College of the Atlantic since 1983 and Susan Bickford teaches at the University of Maine-Augusta. Some not only teach but are heads of departments. Ling-Wen Tsai is head of the sculpture department at Maine College of Art, Susan Groce is chair of the art department at University of Maine, Orono and Celeste Roberge coordinator of the sculpture area at the University of Florida.

In the seventies the cry for equal rights brought, amongst other things, the Equal Rights Amendment, the Supreme Court's 1973 Roe vs. Wade case and *Ms Magazine* (1972). *Take Back the Night* marches against violence and rape began in 1977 in Belgium. Maine held its first in 1980. "We say, No More" was the cry for the end of violence against women. During this era, sometimes referred to as the Second Wave of the Women's movement (the first being the suffragette movement of the 1920s), women asserted their rights and place in the world. MWP III artists have benefited from the fervent feminism of this early political phase with its demands for women to be included in museums and exhibitions, to be recipients of awards and fellowships, to be recognized and taken seriously—to be legitimate. Seeking to find their voice and their place, women marched, demonstrated, wrote manifestoes and organized feminist meetings, protests and exhibits.

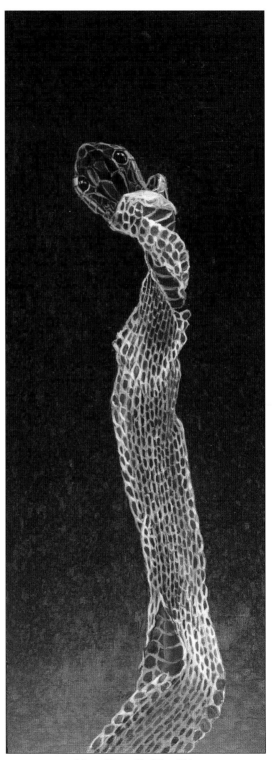

Mary Hart, *Shedding Skin*

MWP III artists have all benefited from these efforts—many of them were active in these demands. Today the MWP III artists are recipients of awards and fellowships and grants including the prestigious Guggenheim awarded to Katherine Bradford in 2011 and Yvonne Jacquette in 1998, the Elaine De Kooning Scholarship in painting awarded to Mary Hart and the Pollock-Krasner Foundation has been awarded to Carrie Scanga in 2008 and twice to Celeste Roberge, once in 1991 and again in 1998. Judy Glickman, in 1993, was awarded a Fellowship of Distinction from the Royal Photographic Society of Great Britain. Lois Dodd is a member of the American Academy of Arts and Letters and the National Academy of Design. Katarina Weslien received an individual grant from the National Endowment of the Arts. On a state and regional level most of the artists in the show have received grants from the Maine Arts Commission.

MWP III artists are no longer taking the backseat as Marguerite Zorach had to do in the thirties and forties for her husband, William Zorach. Most of the MWP III artists are active exhibitors, not only regionally in galleries and museums, but also nationally and internationally. Just as a sampling, Lissa

Ling-Wen Tsai, *Residual*

Hunter's work is in the permanent collection of the Renwick Gallery of the Smithsonian, in Washington D.C., the Museum of Fine Arts and Design in New York and the Museum of Fine Arts in Boston. Dahlov Ipcar, Maine's beloved painter, illustrator, author and daughter of the Zorach's, has work in the Metropolitan Museum, the Whitney and the Brooklyn Museum. Yvonne Jacquette and Lois Dodd also are included in the Met's collection. Rose Marasco's work is held in the permanent collections of Bowdoin, the Fogg Art Museum at Harvard, and the New York Public Library. Ling-Wen Tsai has been exhibiting internationally in Greece, Taiwan, Italy, Germany and Iraq. No longer does a woman have to be nude to get into the Met as the Guerilla Girls quipped back in the 70s, many women are already there, including our own Lois Dodd.

In addition MWP III's artists are active leaders in the art world. While we don't have any museums yet dedicated solely to Maine women artists, like the National Museum of Women in the Arts in Washington D.C. (1987) or the Women's Studio Workshop in Rosendale, New York, women in Maine have founded important institutions. Marylin Quint-Rose founded Maine Women in the Arts. Alice Spencer, Judith Allan-Efstathiou along with Susan Amons and others founded Peregrine Press which has been an important resource for printmakers. The photographers, Denise Froehlich, Melonie Bennett with Elizabeth Moss and Anne Zill, director of the UNE Art Gallery and co-curator for MWP III, founded Maine Museum of Photographic Arts, a virtual museum for photography, film, videography, installations and new media—a first in Maine. Kate Cheney Chappell founded the Kate Cheney Chappell Center for Book Arts at USM of which Rebecca Goodale is currently the director.

Maine Women Pioneers III artists are clearly empowered. Is it perfect? Of course not. No question there is still sexism and discrimination just as there is still gay bashing, anti-Semitism and racism. No doubt there are many times when women are still perceived as the second sex. According to one report women artists make up only 5% of the art currently on display in U.S. museums. So, there is much still to do.

Women artists continue to be all over the map when it comes to their relationship to issues of gender, identity and art. Some see their gender and their experience as a woman as an important piece of their artistic expression, others don't; some seek out historically based female artistic practices, others intentionally avoid that, some feel some have sold out and joined the old boys' network again, while others don't feel that way at all. There is no party line.

In her book, *Feminist Consequences* (2001), Misha Kauka remarked that "Feminism ain't what it used to be." What she observed is that feminism is in a different place than it was in the 1960s and 1970s. There is no clear goal as there use to be, partly because many of the demands of those decades have been improved and assimilated into our culture, and, the cries for social justice have been extended to other marginalized groups such as the gay/lesbian/queer communities as well as to other causes, such as domestic violence and abuse, the environment, endangered species, and sustainability. Feminism has not disappeared, it just has evolved and expanded its quest into ever widening circles.

Kate Cheney Chappell, *Requiem*

MWP III artists explore the gamut of these issues through the venues of post-modern contemporary art—photography, performance, video, interactive installation, digital as well as painting, printmaking, and sculpture. Postmodern artists have broken down many of the traditional categories of art as well as explored a wide range of new subjects and materials. Feminism has played a role in that shake-up and exploration as well. Eleanor Heartney, Helaine Posner, Nancy Princethal and Sue Scott in their book *After the Revolution* (2007) see how women artists have transformed contemporary art. We can see it in the way MWP III works, which are discussed in the four catalogue essays in depth, that MWP III artists are innovators, activists, visionaries, healers, and veterans with long and distinguished careers who have brought new ideas, forms and media to the forefront of American art today.

MWP III brings honor and recognition to the extraordinary role women artists have played in creating and revolutionizing contemporary art on a regional, national and international level. Like their predecessors in MWP I and II, MWP III demonstrates how women artists continue to be the pioneers if not the revolutionaries of this new era. This exhibition is a cause for celebration.

• • •

JOAN P. URANECK is an art historian and professor at the Maine College of Art where she has taught since 1975 (when it was the Portland School of Art). She is also a scholar of Picasso's early drawings and has published articles in *The Burlington Magazine* and in *Fine Art Connoisseur*. She is a frequent lecturer in the state and wrote the scholarly essay, *Pioneering Aesthetics*, for the 1985 exhibition catalogue, *Women Pioneers in Maine Art: 1900–1945*.

SELECTED BIBLIOGRAPHY

Nochlin, Linda, "Why Have There Been No Great Women Artists?" *Art News*, January 1971, pp. 22–39, 67–71.

Heartney, Eleanor, Helaine Posner, Nancy Princethal and Sue Scott. *After the Revolution: Women Who Transformed Contemporary Art*, New York: Prestel, 2007.

Elisabeth Bronfen & Misha Kavka, editors. *Feminist.* Consequences. New York: Columbia University Press, New York, 2001.

WHY AN EXHIBITION OF WOMEN ARTISTS IN 2012?

Edgar Allen Beem

Back in 1981, when the Joan Whitney Payson Gallery of Art at Westbrook College (now the University of New England Art Gallery) mounted *Women Pioneers in Maine Art*, no one would have questioned the rationale for an exhibition of 19th women artists.

Even a few years later in 1985, when the gallery organized *Women Pioneers in Maine Art 1900–1945*, the justification for an all-women exhibition of pre-World War II art was perfectly clear. There was an historical bias against women artists that needed to be addressed. A little revisionist history was in order to set the record straight.

The 1981 and 1985 *Maine Women Pioneer* exhibitions were attempts to redress the historical grievances of under-represented and under-appreciated women artists in Maine. After a 27-year hiatus, during which the university, its art gallery and the art world evolved considerably, the UNE Art Gallery has now mounted a third *Maine Women Pioneers* to celebrate the contributions of contemporary women artists to Maine's art heritage. *Maine Women Pioneers III* is the result of more than 150 hours of discussions between and among

gallery director Anne B. Zill, Gael May McKibben, who helped organize the first two exhibitions, and Portland gallerist Andres Azucena Verzosa, who has been lobbying for a contemporary women pioneers exhibition for several years.

As with any group exhibition, one can always argue about who's included and who's not and whether the organizing themes make sense or not, but *Maine Women Pioneers III* begs a larger question—"Is an exhibition of contemporary women artists necessary or justifiable in 2012?"

THE BIAS

To begin with, it is quite clear that no one wants to be thought of as a "woman artist," separate and unequal. Conceptual artist Anna Hepler (b. 1969) makes this post-feminist point most emphatically in explaining why she declined to exhibit in *Maine Women Pioneers III*. "My reasons for declining participation have to do with using gender as an organizing principle," Hepler says. "A show of all women artists seems arbitrary to me in the same way as a show of short artists, or old artists, would be. . . . I am not interested in having my particular physical attributes, or gender used as a required qualification for inclusion."

Gender, of course, has been an historic basis for exclusion. In 1963, for example, when the Colby College Museum of Art published its landmark *Maine and Its Role in American Art, 1740–1963,* the book and the exhibition it documented featured 151 artists, only 12 of whom were women. Curiously, that 8% (12/151) figure is exactly the same percentage of women that inspired a group of anonymous women art professionals in 1985 to found the celebrated Guerrilla Girls, activists who adopt the names of famous women artists and wear gorilla masks to hide their identities as they seek to raise consciousness about art world discrimination against women.

One of the best-known Guerrilla Girls posters depicts a reclining female nude with a gorilla head and asks the question, "Do women have to be naked to get into the Met Museum?" The Guerrilla Girls calculated that women constitute only 5% of the artists exhibited at the Met but 85% of the nudes. "Until recently," says the Guerrilla Girls spokesperson who goes by the name Kathe Kollwitz, "almost every museum was filled with art by white males, plus one or two token women and artists of color. Due to the work of the Guerrilla Girls, lots of other tireless agitators and enlightened curators, things have improved a bit. Now there are nine or ten token women and artists of color who get their work shown."

SEXISM AND THE SECOND SEX

Dahlov Ipcar (b. 1917), the only artist in the contemporary *Maine Women Pioneers III* show who was also in the pre–World War II *Maine Women Pioneers* exhibition, has a longer experience of art world politics than most, her father and mother, William and Marguerite Zorach, having been artists before her.

Dahlov Ipcar, *Serengeti Triad*

"In my mother's day," says Ipcar, "she had to take a backseat to my father's career, but she is now becoming recognized as a pioneer in American art." Ipcar suggests it was a patriarchal society, not the family patriarch, that designated her mother as what Simone De Beauvoir called "the second sex."

"My father was pretty appreciative of my mother," she says. "He said she was a better artist than he was. They had a symbiotic relationship. She had much more original ideas and he would develop them."

One *Maine Women Pioneer III* artist who has experienced sexist discrimination is Arla Patch (b. 1950), an artist who often uses images of the female body to evoke divine and healing powers. "I have been keenly aware of my immersion in the patriarchy since my art school days in the late sixties and early seventies as a sculpture major in a nearly all male department," says Patch. "I was subjected to sexual harassment and diminishing by even the professor. A sense of having to 'prove myself' was ever present."

Patch believes men often just don't understand her work, which deals with "embodiment, the divine feminine, and overcoming the 'less than' message of the culture." "I know that these images are powerful and can trigger anyone, male or female, who does not fully inhabit their bodies or has some un-metabolized story embedded in their body," says Patch. Rebecca Goodale (b. 1953), an artist best known for her one-of-a-kind books, says one of the problems for women artists historically has been a lack of role models. As a student at the Portland School of Art in the 1970s, Goodale says "a student really had to dig to come up with some female role models. Even my female art history professors seemed to only lecture about male artists." Goodale, who has taught at the University of Southern Maine for more than 30 years, says most of her students these days are women. "In fact, some semesters they are all women," she says. "The USM Art Department has a large majority of female students and I take this seriously. Now I have a responsibility to be a role model."

"Art schools and university art departments often have over 60% female students," observes Guerrilla Girls spokesperson Kathe Kollwitz. "After school it's a different story: there is still a crushing glass ceiling and most museums of contemporary art have less than 20% women in their collections."

THE LESS THAN FACTOR

It is not uncommon for women artists to feel that they have to work twice as hard as male artists to get the same recognition, that they still have to overcome the "less than" message of our culture.

"It's the same in almost any field and the topic makes me very tired," agrees artist Dozier Bell (b. 1957). "The assumptions of competence, ability, and potential are all against one. It has tended to make me avoid the art world to the extent that I can and stay in the mental bubble I've created for myself with my work." Bell, whose brooding imagery often seeks to give external expression to internal states of mind, finds that unless she is "ingratiating" she is considered "difficult" in business dealings. She also senses a double standard when it comes to taking an artist seriously. "When a woman voices an idea," she says, "it often doesn't get picked up until a man gets behind it, which is galling."

Kate Cheney Chappell (b. 1945), a multimedia artist whose work often evokes

Susan Amons
*Chocolate Lynxs
I, II, III*

natural and organic processes, finds that the social double standard can sometimes be more insidious than overt. "People will say, 'Oh, isn't that lovely, you're an artist. You must enjoy that,' like it's my hobby," Chappell says. "I want to say, 'It's lonely, frustrating, and damn hard work.'"

"'Are you still painting?' That's an even worse one," agrees Alison Hildreth (b. 1934), one of Maine's finest artists and a member of one of the state's most prominent families. Like many woman artists, Alison Hildreth put her art career on hold in order to raise children. She did not have a studio outside the home until she was 43. "I am very aware of the inequities that have existed and am grateful to groups such as the Guerrilla Girls," says Hildreth. "Women artists have benefited from the work of others who confronted this historical bias."

To help overcome this "less than" factor, women artists sometimes find strength in numbers. Kate Cheney Chappell, for instance, is a member of Women Artists of Monhegan and was one of 36 women who exhibited in the 2007 *On Island: Women Artists of Monhegan* exhibition at UNE.

Marylin Quint-Rose (b. 1927) found that early in her long career as a sculptor she

suffered from "being taken less seriously and not having opportunities presented to me."

"I signed my name Quint-Rose because I didn't want my work to be known as woman's art," she says. "I wanted it to stand on its own two feet." Like many women artists, Quint-Rose has found there is strength in numbers. In 1977, Quint-Rose, who works in corrogated paper, founded Maine Women in the Arts.

And Susan Amons (b. 1954) received her "biggest creative break" when she was awarded a printmaking fellowship to the Women's Studio Workshop in Rosendale, New York. She has had 14 WSW residencies over the past 20 years. "I have found," says Amons, "that groups of artists have greater success and visibility than one artist alone, especially when it comes to starting out in a career."

ENLIGHTENED MAINE

Photographer Rose Marasco (b. 1948), whose own work frequently deals with the lives of women, reflects on the progress women artists have made by quoting sculptor Sarah Sze in a recent *New Yorker* profile. Sze, who will represent the United States at the 2013 Venice Biennale, said "one of the freedoms that early feminist artists fought for was freedom from the expectation that a woman makes art about being a woman." "I agree with this very much," says Marasco. "That said, I do not feel the only valid way to make art is to take an activist position to point out wrongs. I admire those who do, but it is simply not who I am. I have chosen both in my work, and my life, to raise up awareness of ordinary women's lives, and in so doing, to hopefully add to the larger dialogue." "I do think," says Marasco, adding an important note, "there is a difference between the Portland art world and the New York City art world."

Alice Spencer (b. 1944) is a key player in the Portland art scene not only because she is an accomplished painter and printmaker but also because she has served on the board of Maine College of Art, chaired the City of Portland's Public Art Committee, and co-founded the Peregrine Press. Spencer believes more doors are open to women artists in Maine in part because "the small scale of the Maine arts community, the necessity for cooperation over competition among galleries and museums, the fact that women hold many of the arts administrative jobs in the state…and have created a climate of access for women artists in the state."

THE PROS OF BEING A WOMEN ARTIST

The historical bias against women in art may not yet have been entirely overcome, but Alice Spencer thinks contemporary women artists can draw strength from past adversity. Spencer believes "women artists are, in general, advantaged. They are privileged by their immediate past history and are building on the gains of the previous vanguard. They are becoming more certain of their self-worth and more savvy as marketers."

Photographer Keliy Anderson-Staley (b. 1977), one of the youngest artists in the *Maine Women Pioneers III* series, manifests gender in some of her work by incorporating hand-knit doilies, embroidered lace, other heirloom objects that speak to "how we make history, especially personal and family history, out of objects and photographs." Anderson-Staley says she has run into "an old boys' network" in the photography world, but women have helped her overcome it. "My work shows in a number of galleries and, coincidently perhaps, they are all run by women. In the gallery world there are certainly a number of female power-brokers, and it has been a pleasure to work with some of them. In my own experience, women gallery owners are more likely to give shows to women artists than male gallery owners are."

Melonie Bennett (b. 1969), who has become one of Maine's most celebrated artists for her intimate photographs of family life and country life, believes being a woman provides her access. "It kind of helps me in situations where people feel less intimidated by a woman," says Bennett. The role she plays in her large, bumptious family puts people at ease and provides her entré. "I take care of everyone and make everyone feel comfortable," says Bennett. "It's the caretaker role. I'm always the peacemaker."

Sculptor Celeste Roberge (b. 1951) says coming of age in the 1970s she was inspired by artists such as Louise Bourgeois, Eva Hesse, Jackie Winsor, and Lee Bonticou. Describing herself as "a feminist from birth," Roberge has never allowed being a *woman* to become an obstacle. "If anything," she says, "it motivated me to work harder and not stop."

Abby Shahn (b.1940) sees herself as bridging the gap between the pre-feminist artists of the 1950s and feminist artists of the 1970s. Shahn believes that women artists of her generation were often too competitive and unsupportive of other women artists because they were trying to win the approval of a male-dominated art world. "I like hanging out with a lot of younger women," says Shahn. "Younger women seem more free of that lack of self-respect."

And finally, while Lauren Fensterstock (b. 1975) confesses to "mixed emotions" about an all-women art show, she embraces the idea in the spirit of creative inquiry. "I don't think my gender defines me, but it is an aspect that shapes my perspective," says Fensterstock, whose cut paper garden installations evince the feminine both materially and botanically. Fensterstock has, however, experienced the art world double standard. When her partner Aaron Stephan

decided to stop taking outside work in order to focus on his art, their families, friends and colleagues all said, "Of course." But when Fensterstock recently decided to resign her position as academic director of the Maine College of Art MFA program, many people cautioned her not to quit her day job.

Fensterstock ignored the advice. She has been successful at everything she has ever done; why wouldn't she be successful at what she really wants to do. That's a position just about every woman artist has found themselves in at one time or another. "I always joke that my secret to success is 90% brute force and 10% cleavage," says Fensterstock irreverently. "Passion, persistence, and hard work are the center of a career, but I think you need to temper that with some humor and the ability to not take yourself too seriously."

Passion, persistence, and hard work are exactly what justify and are rewarded by *Maine Women Pioneers III*.

• • •

EDGAR ALLEN BEEM is the author of *Maine Art Now* and co-editor of the forthcoming *Maine Art New: Contemporary Art in Maine, 1990 to Now*. He is a freelance writer and art critic who lives in Yarmouth, Maine and has been writing about art in Maine since 1978.

VANGUARD

TIMELY AND TIMELESS DIALOGUES
AT THE EDGE OF TODAY

Britta Konau

Women artists have a vibrant often leading presence in new media, initially photography and more recently video and performance art among them. These new disciplines come without the ideological baggage of male-dominated tradition and thus supply a level playing field. Not surprisingly, the nine artists in the Vanguard section of *Maine Women Pioneers III* engage in mostly non-traditional media and often work across disciplines, participating in the current trend of abolishing specialization in a particular medium. All of them are extremely innovative and constantly push their medium, and themselves, to further the dialogue that is the art of today. They happen to live in Maine at the moment, some even grew up here, but their vision, experience, and rigorous professional practice is of a national and international level.

Ling-Wen Tsai works in photography, video, drawing, painting, installation, and performance art, often combined or collaboratively. Since coming to the U.S. from Taiwan, Tsai has experienced what she calls "in-between-ness," a state of dislocation and heightened perception that she has lately applied to investigations of the constitutive elements of the world—water, sound, movement, wind, and time.

For participants in *Sitting Quietly* the inner noise of our thinking takes over. But the sensory deprivation, which the noise-reduction headsets provide, also provides a contemplative space. As a communal event, the work may cause an inherent discomfort by breaking our Western imperative to communicate, and instead, encouraging shared silence. How long can we stand not doing anything other than being, in isolation or society? What is the value of communication?

The installation embodies utmost restraint and shares its palette with Tsai's drawings. In a careful balance between chance and control, the artist applies sumi ink to partially wetted paper, letting material and gravity affect the outcome. The results are atmospheric interactions between emptiness and clusters of darkness, not unlike the sensory aspects of *Sitting Quietly*. Both works exist at the threshold of experience, guiding our view inward, toward reflection, silence, and imagination. With her controlled environments in support of open-ended experience, Tsai invites slowing down and paying attention to our experience of the world so that we may not mistake it for granted and its distractions as inevitable.

Lihua Lei has heroically used her own physical disability caused by polio she contracted as a toddler to communicate her beliefs on what it means to be human. In her installations and performances, human biological rhythms intersect with nature's forces, symbolizing humanity's cyclical nature from birth to death.

Lihua Lei,
Inner Piece (detail)

Acting like memento mori, the unfired clay figures in Lei's *Inner Piece* embody the vulnerability of body and mind as the outer earthen mantle disintegrates over time to reveal a translucent core of layered papier-mâché, epoxy, and Himalayan salt. This interior form symbolizes our inner light that Lei believes we all share as a connective energy. If we paid enough attention, this gradual transformation to reveal our common sacred nature would be apparent to us all. With *Inner Piece* Lei has transcended her source of inspiration from the personal to the universal, from a focus on bodily and psychological confinement and expansion to a release of spiritual energy.

Susan Bickford's interactive and immersive art environments utilize advanced technology, including motion sensors, feedback and immersion video, animation, and sound, as well as old-fashioned analog devices, thus embodying a continuum of technology and time that is imbued with content.

In *Torndado* the brutality and ominous physicality of a motorized bone cutter and a hand-cranked drill clash with the immateriality of electronic media and projections. Visitors become participants as their motion activates and/or alters the visual and auditory imagery playing out on their bodies. *Torndado*'s set-up evokes indoor and outdoor space in which the flitting shapes and shadows and enveloping sound are dramatically more beautiful than the devices producing them, creating a shift in aesthetic between causal and resultant elements. Bickford intentionally leaves her installations' workings visible so that they can feel like makeshift laboratories. The complex interconnectedness between the immaterial and the physical is meant to reflect how the world is similarly interconnected and cyclical in nature. Human effect on the artworks' content serves as a metaphor for our impact on the environment. Bickford's works are also steeped in personal experience, resulting in intriguing yet slightly hermetic narratives.

Amy Stacey Curtis thinks big. Since 2000, she has created large-scale temporary multi-part installations every two years in empty mill spaces all over Maine. Each consisting of nine individual installations, they have tackled successively more conceptual themes of perception including experience, change, and light, and will end in 2016 with memory. The installations are made of

simple materials ranging from wood, glass, and metal, to sound and video which are fashioned into geometric shapes in multiples of nine and require the participation of visitors for completion. Autobiographical elements are often incorporated and all display decisions are based on the artist's own height.

SPACE is the seventh installment and occupies three floors of the Winthrop Commerce Center (formerly Carleton Woolen Mill). Themes explored encompass expanse, direction, volume, capacity, and place. Guiding participants through instructions from a passive, verbal, and rational state to an active, physical or perceptual, and experiential engagement allows them to contemplate space in new ways.

Throughout Curtis' biennials, chaos, order, and repetition surface as concerns. More specifically, she explores the confluence and disparity of individual perception and experience as it is expressed in rhythms of length, time, and speed among other parameters, thus revealing difference within commonality. As a basic aspect of being human, this relativity subtly illustrates the artist's concept that we are part of a whole.

Julie Poitras Santos creates installations incorporating methods of divination and ritualistic performances. Evoking associations with ancient archetypes or tableaux of mystery plays, the scenarios allow for a temporary removal from our ordinary context to envision a parallel space of exploration and transformation.

The complex installation *twist (when one wonders what)* extends over two levels and encompasses objects, video projection, sound, and intermittent performances. The most prominent element, a snake-like tangle of black ropes, is being unraveled by a performer who is perched like a crow on a high stool, wearing a black feather jacket. The set-up brings to mind the subconscious or world of dreams below, from which the rope, like a scrambled narrative or thought, emerges to be untangled and made comprehensible. But the rope is actually being un-twisted, its history and defining characteristic undone, in a move toward abstracted essences. The work's focus on creation and its undoing on multiple levels of interpretation also extends to the space it inhabits and reflects, succinctly symbolized by a little feathered house.

Working exclusively with paper, **Carrie Scanga** pushes the limits of her medium in drawings, prints, sculptures and installations. Valuing paper for its inherent purpose as a carrier of meaning and function, the artist often breaks away from its two-dimensionality. In brick-like

ABOVE: **Julie Poitros Santos**, *twist (when one wonders what)* (detail)

constructions of tracing paper, gravity and the delicacy of the medium are allowed to transform the sculpture over time. All of her pieces explore mnemonic and relational functions of space for the individual.

Seasonal is a series of images of booths, shacks, and tents that combines straight-edged architectural drawing with playful shapes and lusciously liquid coloration. Some works leave the strict plane of two dimensions behind by incorporating collaged elements. As comments on the transitional nature of our environment these works highlight the arbitrariness of assigning value to any structure. The buildings are disquietingly unmoored from any surroundings, being anchored only by the architecture of the paper itself. The artist's lightness of touch floats the structures as disembodied as memories, turning them into anticipatory spaces to be narratively completed.

Lauren Fensterstock's work occupies a position of contradictions—romantic and ominous, excessive and minimalist, conceptual and blatantly emotional. She explores her subjects from many different directions, evidencing a highly curious and complex thinking process behind her meticulously crafted objects.

Since 2007, Fensterstock has explored the nature/culture relationship in the series *Third Nature*—a Renaissance term for shaping nature for aesthetic pleasure, including garden design. Nowadays though, the term also includes representations of nature and acknowledges that nature has become a simulacrum of itself. Fensterstock has combined her study of European garden design with an ambivalent appreciation of the monumentality of the works and egos involved in Earth Art, and with 19th-century women's handicrafts. In an extremely labor intensive process, she quills black paper into intricate botanically accurate or fantastical flowers and plants. Embedded in dusky mounts of charcoal, her work is either displayed in shallow, glass-fronted wall cases or as large floor installations. In either case, reflections on the glass or embedded Plexiglas panels pierce the coherence of the work and allow for a variable dialogue with the surroundings. The works' aesthetic of excess intriguingly resonates with associations of death, night and disappearance.

Instead of exuberant flowers, *A Selection of Ground and Surface* contains bundles of grass in charcoal soil. Its visible layering resembles an archaeological cross section or a natural history display, thus introducing a sense of authenticity and authority that is immediately invalidated by the work's evident artifice. The triptych's horizontality evokes an expansive view of a post-apocalyptic desert. This sublimely dystopian transformation of nature is portable nature, constructed, and devoid of life—yet fabulously beautiful too. Fensterstock's works encourage an emotional ambiguity that may be close to understanding the toll our current pace of living has taken on the environment.

In **Diana Cherbuliez**'s sculptures, edgy imagination goes hand in hand with amazing craftsmanship. Driven by ideas and exquisite sensitivity to materiality and technique, every factor contributing to the final work has been carefully chosen for its relevance, allusion, tradition, and beauty. With a dark humor and sense of the absurd, Cherbuliez draws on fairy tales and other stories for inspiration, but also addresses personal and social concerns. Her materials are mostly found or stem from her own life, including hair and dust from under her bed. She seems able to make anything her slightly wicked imagination can dream up—chemically softened wishbones twist into a Möbius strip, apples have faces carved into them, cigarette butts form a hand grasping its own tail.

Mirrors recur frequently in the artist's work as emblems of reflection but also futility. Extending any structure or object in front of them, they can generate infinity or labyrinths. Human hair is loaded with associations, among them the obvious of beauty as well as narrative, memorial, and social functions. Formed into a rope or intricately braided, it becomes a symbol of strength and vulnerability at the same time. It seems that Cherbuliez is always capable to see myriad sides to the dilemma of being in the world.

Behind the deadpan character of **Alicia Eggert**'s kinetic sculptures lurks opportunity for contemplative engagement. The work that is thematically centered on time envisions a state of always being in-between. The time never seems to be right yet that is all we have—it is always right. At the same time, it is never now and it is always now. And of course we are always dying from the moment we are born.

We all face consciously or unconsciously, voluntarily or not, these profound puzzles, questions, and realizations concerning our very existence. Eggert's representations of various models of perceiving and conceiving of time are realized with commonplace objects and in your face, in a language that we know from modern urban environments, but they subtly needle us.

As much as these nine artists are looking toward the future in their use of media and technology, they are also, without exception, addressing timeless subjects. Their work reflects a profundity of thought that asks questions artists have posed for centuries: How do we inhabit the world? How do we understand it? And, phrased in contemporary lingo yet no less ancient, how can we maintain our humanity and spirituality in the onslaught of information, competitive struggle, and environmental and ecological instability. The artists do not provide answers to these questions. Answers seem to belong to a previous time when certainty was claimed possible. But they do contribute stimulating starting points for introspection.

• • •

BRITTA KONAU is an independent art writer, critic, and curator.

I am working with electronic media and interaction within immersive installation. I have come to understand my art making as a capsule of collaborative attention which can make apparent emerging relationships. This kind of interactivity involves calling my viewers to be present and to make something happen. I have a deep interest in the natural world as it is an immersive and responsive system. I am working with interactive systems because it is my hope that through experiencing my art people will recognize their impact on the world around them. Choices we make change the world around us but sometimes we can't see the results of our actions. We don't make connections. It is my intention to accentuate the connections to make them more visible.

Tornadado, immersive installation, interactive video, sound and electronic sculpture, 2012. Courtesy the University of New England Art Gallery.

PHOTOGRAPH BY LUC DEMERS

While my sculpture is largely conceptual, it remains rooted in the poetry of materials—their specific physical beauty, history, and references. In my current work, ladders and bridges are structures of transition that give shape to other ambiguous states, like the drift between consciousness and sleep. Constructed from salvaged building materials and collected refuse of my own life, the works' subject, media, and methods all inform the project to make visible the latent connections between the things we use in our daily lives and who we have been and will be.

PHOTOGRAPH BY LUC DEMERS

Ahem, construction-waste plywood and walnut, glass, mirror, and anonymous hair, 10.25" x 10.25" x 10.25".
Courtesy the University of New England Art Gallery.

My interactive installations physically exist as art when temporarily assembled in a space and experienced by an audience. Without the audience's careful participation, my installations are static, literally incomplete. Many of my installations require participants' physical touch, effect, or perpetuation while others function through active and purposeful perspective. Each installation includes instructions, an integral part of the experience. Participants change, maintain, enter, distinguish, becoming part of each installation and the exhibit as a whole. Following each exhibit, these works exist only through documentation, dialogue, and memory.

place (from SPACE, Curtis' seventh solo-biennial), installation, .25" x 297" x 807", 2012.

Alicia Eggert is an artist whose work commonly takes the form of kinetic, interactive, and time-based sculpture. Due to earning bachelor's degree in interior design, receiving a graduate degree in sculpture, and having a sincere interest in dance and mechanics, her art practice is extremely interdisciplinary in nature. The body of work chosen for *MWP III* represents a primary focus in Alicia's work: illustrating the different ways that we perceive and understand time. One kinetic sculpture repeatedly creates and destroys *NOW*; another reveals the hidden mathematics of life. Cyclical and linear, finite and infinite representations of time are juxtaposed. Change is the only constant.

NOW, 2012, DC motor, Arduino microcontroller, timing belts & pulleys, acrylic, plywood, mixed media, 48" x 72" x 12". Made with help from Alexander Reben.

My recent work draws from my research into three disparate practices: the pleasure and refinement of ladies' accomplishments of the 18th century; the high-minded machismo of American Earth Art in the 20th century; and the socially complex evolution of French and English garden design of the 16th–18th centuries. Practitioners in each of these fields developed highly stylized forms to express their ideologies and social aspirations, often going to extraordinary lengths to create something *natural*. I bring together elements from each of these disciplines to expose their frivolities, contradictions and purposefully constructed features. Through combination I hope to bring attention to the variety of sources spanning centuries, continents, and gender roles that collectively merge to shape the peculiarities of a personal vantage point.

A Selection of Ground and Surface (detail), 2010, paper and charcoal behind glass, 15' x 1'.
Courtesy Aucocisco Galleries, Portland, Maine.

Throughout our very temporary existence, we are subject to the biological processes of conception, growth, and maturation and eventually decay. We are all born as singular individuals and we all die as such. In our lifetimes though, most of us desire to love and be loved and to connect to others. This installation is an outdoor, time/space, performance/installation piece composed of several clay objects set outside where exposure to the weather will complete the piece through natural erosion. Like all of us, the installation will not be the same one day as it will be the next, and no one can precisely predict how time and the elements will shape it. What is left behind when time, gravity and the elements have their way?

PHOTOGRAPH BY LUC DEMERS

Inner Piece, 2012, mixed media: clay, Hymalya salt, paper maché, epoxy, solar light, polycarbonate bases. Courtesy the University of New England Art Gallery.

JULIE POITRAS SANTOS

Julie Poitras Santos creates temporary works of site-specific performance, and installations using a diversity of media. Through research and dialogue, and by looking to divinatory methods, her work regards the potential for ritual gesture to create a separate place between known territories, allowing space for new narratives to be created. In lacing together site, memory, and local mythologies the work explores our desire for both belonging and difference through the stories we interpret and the stories we tell.

twist (when one wonders what) (detail), 2012, rope, video, sound, paint, wooden stool, feather jacket, performer (intermittent), installation, video still.
Courtesy the University of New England Art Gallery.

My exploration is concerned with space, the intimacy of individual experience and the luminal aspects of memory. Buildings and cultural myths both are terrains that become saturated with people's stories through use and circulation. Working in two dimensions, I have developed my own hybrid of drawing/painting/printmaking, in which I intuitively re-work the paper until a space and story emerge.

My installations reflect my life-long interest in the relationship between our internal physical sense of occupying bodies and our perceptions of occupying architectural space. I push the delicate material of tracing paper to its limit, relying on its folds to lend stability to forms. Over the course of an exhibit, the paper eventually gives way to gravity, and at the exhibit's closing, the work is recycled.

PHOTOGRAPH BY LUC DEMERS

Mountain Invention, 2012, graphite, gouache and drypoints on paper, 60" x 22" x 1.5".
Courtesy the University of New England Art Gallery.

M y work is a response to observations of everyday life. In our sensory-overload, media-saturated environment, I strive to create experiences that allow time-space for the viewer to engage with their own seeing and listening. Drawing attention to ever-present phenomena, I invite the viewer into a state of reflection where one is left with the "self."

PHOTOGRAPH BY MIKE FLEMING

Sitting Quietly, 2012, seven stools, seven noise reduction headsets, and one pendant light, dimension variable.

HOMAGE

HOMAGE AND THE SPACE OF ENGAGEMENT

Carl Little

"Homage" derives from the French word for man—*homme*—and, in its earliest usage, represented a declaration of fealty to a feudal lord. Over the centuries the word has evolved away from its gender-based, socio-economic origins. When we pay homage today, we salute individual achievement, often the kind realized over an extended period, if not a lifetime.

Homage may take many forms: a critical appreciation, a *festschrift*, an act of emulation. In this case, an exhibition serves as tribute, to a baker's dozen of master artists who, the discerning curators state, provide "powerful examples of career and lifelong original creative accomplishment" and who are, furthermore, situated "ahead of the curve without resting on their laurels."

Take **Beverly Hallam** (b. 1923): in the 1950s, this artist from York was a pioneer in the use of polyvinyl acetate, the medium we now call acrylic. She created abstract

Alison Hildreth,
Emerging Cartographies

constructions and demonstrated the technique to fellow artists. Restless to innovate, she moved to monotype and then mastered airbrush, the technique used to create the floral pieces that turn our heads to this day.[1] Laurels be damned, Hallam seemed to say at the dawn of the new millennium, as she explored computer graphics, producing a stunning body of abstract-geometric work.

Maggie Foskett (b. 1919) of Camden has an equally innovative sense of aesthetics. In her photographic work Foskett harks back to such pioneer 19th-century camera artists as Anna Atkins and William Fox Talbot. Employing a variation of *cliché verre*, she seeks to create images that suggest, in her words, "how delicate our balance with mortality is."[2] Her response to war, environmental degradation and other issues are at once poetic and forthright.

Another inveterate taker of new paths, Portland-based **Alison Hildreth**

(b. 1934) has drawn inspiration from a wide range of sources, including natural history, ancient maps, and contemporary European literature. "I think we try hard to connect the isolated bits of knowledge that we accumulate in any way we can," Hildreth notes. She has made those connections through paintings, drawings, prints and other means. Her solo show *The Feathered Hand*, mounted at the University of New England Art Gallery in 2010 presented an astonishing multi-medium installation that lifted her metaphysical vision to new realms.[3]

Hildreth maintains a work space in the Bakery Studios in Portland, a hub of creative energy where one can also find Frankie Odom, Deedee Schwartz, Alice Spencer and **Katarina Weslien** (b. 1952). This last-named artist is known for a variety of compelling projects, from a series of prints based on road repair lines in Portland to stop-action films that incorporate still images and video clips with provocative sound accompaniment. Weslien's cross-disciplinary work responds to history, philosophy, religion and other subjects, exploring new ways of viewing and representing the world.[4]

Artist **Susan Groce** (b. 1954), who works out of a studio in Martinsville near Port Clyde, first caught the attention of the Maine art scene with an exhibition at this venue, then called the Joan Whitney Payson Gallery of Art, in 1987. Large-scale architectonic graphite pieces in that show led *Maine Times* critic Edgar Allen Beem to call

Lissa Hunter, *Fern*

the display a "bravura performance."[5] Since then, Groce has continued to develop her ambitious vision, studying "the provisional nature of matter" through such large-scale works as *Invasive Species* (2008).

As in any gathering of diverse visions, connections will be made—of sensibility, of thematic focus. One example: Groce's *Milkweed* and **Lissa Hunter's** *Fern* make for a felicitous pairing, each artist focusing on the inherent beauty of natural forms. Working out of a studio in Portland, Hunter (b. 1945) has pioneered papermaking, fabric and basketry techniques—and enjoys combining mediums to fresh effect.[6] Hunter might be speaking for all the artists in *Homage* when she states, "The only thing I truly know about being an artist is that I must evolve continually, deepening my practice through intentional experience and engagement with process."

Marylin Quint-Rose (b. 1927) from Tenants Harbor shares Hunter's fascination with paper, using it to fabricate sculptures and collages, often abstract, sometimes fanciful. Using such non-traditional materials as egg crates, hemp twine and archival corrugation, she creates expressive objects that are part Nancy Graves, part John Chamberlain, yet which have their own signature presence.

Portland photographer **Rose Marasco** (b. 1948) often works in series, obsessively pursuing a theme or format. From her haunting studies of Maine grange halls to intimate still-life diary "portraits," she offers resonant visions of the quotidian. And she is inventive: while evoking the cut-outs of an earlier era, her silhouette pieces are thoroughly modern. She has managed to further the vision of Berenice Abbott and other pioneers of American photography.[7]

Marylin Quint-Rose,
Celadon Voyage

All of these artists are a part of communities, be it educational institutions—the University of Maine, Maine College of Art, Skowhegan School of Painting and Sculpture—collectives such as the Peregrine Press, or geographic locales. They are independent yet they interact with a host of others. Many mentor, others collaborate—all are committed to engaging us with their visions.

Monhegan Island has been spirit central for **Frances Kornbluth** (b. 1920) since 1959. In a line that includes Reuben Tam, Lawrence Goldsmith and Elena Jahn, Kornbluth has employed abstract-expressionist means to create lyric visions, including cloudscapes and tidal tone poems. "I have been recording and communicating a continuum concerned with the natural order of things," she explains, "in a realm where details have a life of their own and often dictate new patterns that expand meaning and the boundaries of personal experience."

Another island, Georgetown, became the home of **Dahlov Ipcar** (b.1917) in 1937; she continues to live and paint there today. Her earliest work related to farm animals—chickens, bulls, draft horses—but as she developed as an artist, her menagerie went global.[8] She also invented: her cloth sculptures are among the earliest of their kind. "Artists," she says, "should create new visions, not just repeat reality"—a credo borne out in the work in *Homage*.

Lois Dodd (b. 1927) and **Yvonne Jacquette** (b. 1934) arrived in Maine's midcoast around the same time, in the 1950s, as part of a distinguished cadre of artists who ended up setting down deep seasonal roots in that region. They responded to the landscape. Dodd, who eventually found a home in Cushing, was drawn to a variety of motifs, from cows and quarries to houses on fire and lunar eclipses. Jacquette, in Searsmont, took to the air to study farms and nuclear power plants. They have continued to explore: the former, to paraphrase critic Hilton Kramer, reinvented the motif of the figure in the landscape.[9] The latter created reverse constellations: bits of light spied from a helicopter hovering over nighttime Maine.

The printmaking community garnered long-deserved attention in 2006 with the all-state *Maine Print Project* and its related publication, *The Imprint of Place: Maine Printmaking 1800–2005*, by art historian David P. Becker.[10] Several artists in *Homage*

are featured in the book, including Ipcar, Hildreth, Hallam, Dodd, Jacquette, Groce, and **Frances Hodsdon.**

Hodsdon (b. 1926), who has a printmaking studio in Jefferson, specializes in lithography. As Becker noted, this print medium has had few practitioners—the expertise and cost have proven prohibitive. While be-

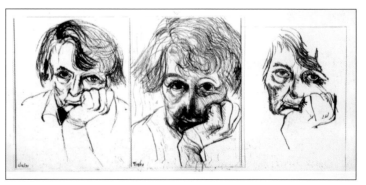

Frances Hodsdon, *Death and Memory #28*

ing the go-to printer for lithographic work, Hodsdon is active in her own explorations of many print mediums, including screen, relief and etching. They offer her "the freedom to experiment with imagery," be it an expressive self-portrait or a ghostly chair.

In this remarkable exhibition thirteen artists demonstrate their dedication to the creative act, to activating what Katarina Weslien has called a "space of engagement." To play on Dante, "Take faith, all who enter here"—and be prepared to engage.

• • •

CARL LITTLE is the author of books on Beverly Hallam, Dorothy Eisner, Dahlov Ipcar and other artists. He lives and writes on Mount Desert Island.

ENDNOTES

1. Beverly Hallam: Artist as Innovator. Maine Masters series (video), 2011.

2. Carolanne Bonanno, Interview with Maggie Foskett. National Museum of Women in the Arts, Sept. 2009, http://womeninthearts. wordpress.com/2009/09/18/artist-spotlight-%E2%80%93-interview-with-maggie-foskett

3. "The three-story space is transformed into a kind of theater of metaphysics." Carl Little, "Alison Hildreth: The Feathered Hand," *Art New England*, March-April, 2011.

4. Weslien has also contributed to the discussion of contemporary aesthetics through her writings and interviews with such artists as Marina Abramovic and Alison Knowles.

5. Edgar Allen Beem, *Maine Art Now.* Gardiner, Maine: Dog Ear Press, 1990, pp. 266-267.

6. Janet Koplos and Bruce Metcalf. *Makers: A History of American Studio Craft.* University of North Carolina Press, 2010.

7. "Rose Marasco: Projections." Houston Center of Photography, 2010. http://hcponline.org/gallery. asp?pageid=12&galid=135.

8. Carl Little, "Maine's Veterans of Painting: Brenda Bettinson, Beverly Hallam and Dahlov Ipcar." *Art New England*, Dec-Jan 2010.

9. "It is as if the artist had set herself the task of reinventing the entire genre of nudes-in-a-landscape out of her own experience in half a century of summers in Maine." Hilton Kramer, "Dodd's Enchanting Nudes: Manhattan Meets Maine." *New York Observer*, August 13, 2001.

10. David P. Becker, *The Imprint of Place: Maine Printmaking 1800–2005.* Camden, Maine: Down East Books, 2006.

My major contact with the out-of-doors is as an observer. I have been a landscape painter from the time I first visited Maine in the early 1950s. While I also work from drawings and paintings in my studio, I continue to paint directly from the landscape, where the instability of weather and the continuously transforming quality of light provides a sense of urgency to an otherwise peaceful and very quiet activity. I neither hunt, fish, nor swim, but will hike some distance carrying portable painting equipment to reach a good spot in which to paint. I am passionate about the beauty of ovals and rectangles and their relationships in nature and on my canvas. I feel I am following an endlessly exciting visual road, both figuratively and sometimes actually, which is the path of my life.

Blanket and Its Shadow at Noon, 1995, oil on panel, 11.75"x 14".
Courtesy Caldbeck Gallery, Rockland, Maine.

Photography makes visible the real and the unreal. Everyone carries a camera, to do what? Preserve a memory? Stop the clock? The possibilities are endless for we live in a universe of change. Around the globe, we have seen the Far Reaches of outer space.

Below the crust of the earth, in a sunless trench deeper than the floor of the ocean, strange fish have been captured on camera. To take a photograph, any photograph, is to follow an engaged curiosity.

An Untitled Space, 1981, Cibachrome, 19.5" x 12.5".
Courtesy Caldbeck Galleries, Rockland, Maine.

Often my work explores the provisional nature of matter—how through environmental time, elemental forces and human activity have so dramatically altered our surroundings. I find it fascinating that such monumental change seems to occur on the very edge of visibility and presence. Consequently in my work, I try to make visible the processes and forces that underpin these changes, forces that are so micro or macroscopic that we fail to notice them on a daily basis.

Polarity, 1995, mixed media drawing, 41.5" x 31.25", series ongoing.

I paint and draw flowers in various sizes and media that offer provocative perspectives on the familiar. I also make colorful digital abstractions. With an airbrush I can study effects such as a light source through petals. After all, a bouquet of flowers is nothing more than a bunch of abstract shapes joined together. Everything realistic is abstract. With digital I discovered a whole new world of making pictures. As the mediums in art change, I change along with them. As Michelangelo said, "I am still learning."

Golden Splendor, 1988, liquitex gesso, acrylic, 36" x 54".

PHOTOGRAPH BY MARY HARDING

I think we try hard to connect the isolated bits of knowledge that we accumulate in any way we can. For me, this process is an exploration in paint, print, drawing, or installation to see if my inquiries, when translated into ever morphing imagery, will allow some kind of pattern to surface. That is the moment in which the work emerges, as if in a novel, with a personality. This is a most provocative, interesting, and challenging time —the point when I have to respect what the work has become.

Bee Keepers, 2001–2, oil collage on linen, 66" x 84".
Courtesy June Fitzpatrick Gallery, Portland, Maine.

Art school and college taught me to do my own printing in all the different printmaking media: screen, relief, lithography, and etching. These techniques are second nature to me. They give me the freedom to experiment with imagery—imagery primarily from my immediate surroundings which builds on ideas and emotions to make connections with nature, self-expression, absurdities and beauty.

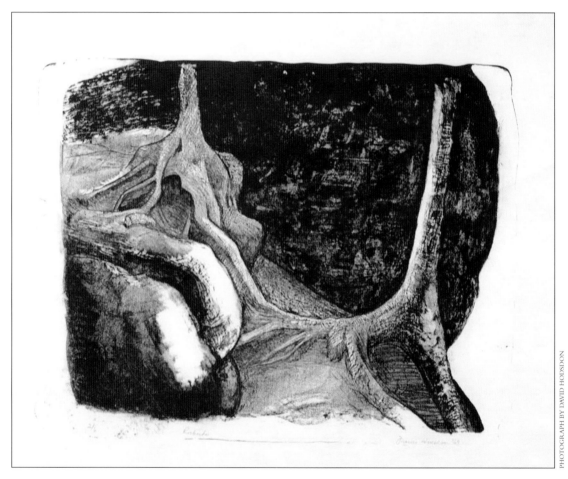

Rockside, edition 2/6, 1969, lithograph stone, 23.5" x 25".

PHOTOGRAPH BY DAVID HODSDON

The only thing I truly know about being an artist is that I must evolve continually, deepening my practice through intentional experience and engagement with process. I am grateful that I still find joy in ideas, knowledge in materials, and the satisfaction of making an object that has some good reason for being in this world.

Bud, Lou, and Monsieur Magritte 2 (detail), 2004, basketry, 2 pieces & 6 apples, 23" x 32" x 14".

PHOTOGRAPH BY K.B. PILCHER

I believe that the most important thing in art is imagination and originality. Artists should create new visions not just repeat reality. Maine is beautiful but I feel inspired to paint new and different worlds.

St. George and the Dragon, 1970, soft sculpture, mixed media, 15" x 32" x 7".
Collection of Charles Ipcar.

A flight to San Diego in 1969 sparked Yvonne Jacquette's interest in aerial views, after which she began flying in commercial airliners to study cloud formations and weather patterns. She soon started sketching and painting the landscape as seen from above, beginning a process that has developed into a defining element of her art. Her first nocturnal painting with an aerial perspective, *East River View at Night* of 1978, inspired an ongoing exploration of the effects of bright lights, reflections, and indistinct objects set against surrounding darkness.

After a trip to Hong Kong in 1990, she began incorporating composite viewpoints into her work, realizing that she could better express the city's many layers of complexity by creating new spatial configurations through multiple perspectives. The resulting pastels and paintings are among her most abstract.

Walmart and Other "Big Box" Stores, Augusta, ME II (detail), 2006, oil on canvas, 58" x 69.75".
Courtesy DC Moore Gallery, New York, New York.

In my art I define and redefine landscape, arriving at abstractions of the natural and man-made environment. My vocabulary of shapes and forms has developed over the years. In recent years, due to a gradual loss of vision, it has become necessary to limit my palette to black and white. Being both observer and participant in rural northeast Connecticut and on a remote island off the coast of Maine, I am constantly challenged to make order out of the impact and complexity of what I know and what I constantly discover. I have been recording and communicating a continuum concerned with the natural order of things, in a realm where details have a life of their own and often dictate new patterns that expand meaning and the boundaries of personal experience

Germination, 1974, acrylic on handmade paper, 28" x 42".

I am exhibiting selected work from three photographic projects that emphasize the role of women in their everyday lives.

Ritual & Community: The Maine Grange (1990–1992) is a selection from my 100 grange exteriors. Vernacular architecture, the secrets of the ritual and community, and the major role women played in the grange, are all aspects of this work.

The Diary Series (1994–2000) is a group of large format color cibachrome prints. Each woman's diary is open to a page incorporating the same dates and, where I have placed an object of note discussed in the diary.

Silhouettes (2010–ongoing) consists of a hand-cut dress shape overlaid onto a famous NYC architectural site or building from the corresponding time period, juxtaposing the private and public sphere.

Silverware Diary, 1998, Cibachrome print, 16" x 20".

As a sculptor working in paper, my intent is to transform appropriated materials into two-dimensional works and to enlarge the scope of each and transform its identity. My work oftentimes employs a special type of selectivity in the use of materials. This is very important in the work itself. Lately, my thoughts wander into global areas, expanding my choice of materials and likewise challenging my choices of both visual aspects and creativity.

Daimon's Choice, 1958, mixed media with leaves, 10.5" x 9.75".
Pittsfield Art Museum, Bertha K. Barstow Award, First Prize, 1958.

My work is multi-disciplinary, taking form in cross-media installation, video, photography, collaborative efforts, books and printmaking. I'm interested in moments of radical transformation, the place where one thing can quickly become something else—the space where the known becomes the strange and where dislocation of what we know presents an unfamiliar familiarity. I wonder about what is important in this cultural moment, what needs to be said, what needs to be made. I believe in the power of simple embodied gestures, subtle shifts, nuance, magnification, hesitation, and gaps. All have the potential to become tools for a space of engagement.

When We Walk We Talk, 1984, cut and woven painting.

WORLDVIEW

WITH OPEN EYES:
ELEVEN ARTISTS VIEW THE WORLD

Agnes Bushell

"When the eye sees something beautiful," Wittgenstein says, "the hand wants to draw it." This sentence is itself so beautiful that Elaine Scarry copies it into her own essay *On Beauty and Being Just*. But before we can reproduce Beauty we must first pause to look at it. "The first flash of the bird," Scarry writes, "incites the desire to duplicate not by translating the glimpsed image into a drawing or a poem or a photograph but simply by continuing to see her . . . as long as the bird is there to behold." Beautiful birds can stop us dead in our tracks if we allow ourselves to notice them. Once we do notice, we find our capacity for seeing other things increases. We find we are paying more attention, not only to the beautiful bird in flight, but to the tree in which it perches, the wetlands in which it nests. Caring for the continued existence of the beautiful bird seems to make us more alert to any threat to it, and ultimately increases our concern and our awareness of the world in which we live.

All eleven artists whose work appears in *Maine Women Pioneers III: Worldview* are passionately engaged with the world and concerned with its fate. For some, the world enters their art as a call to justice, or as a passion to document the time in which they live. For others, the world they view every day is a world of beauty under threat. All of them live in the world with their eyes open. Seeing as they do, their work opens our eyes as well.

Since 2000, **Rebecca Goodale** has been making exquisite, one-of-a-kind artist's books dedicated to threatened and endangered animals and plants in the state of

Rebecca Goodale (in collaboration with Carrie Scanga), *Two or Three Friends*

Maine. In this work, by using folded paper and pen and pencil, Goodale has recreated the beautiful bird of Scarry's essay, and not only the beautiful bird, but the beautiful wild flower, the beautiful butterfly, the beautiful sedge. Art historian Linda J. Docherty compares Goodale's *Threatened and Endangered* to Rachel Carson's *Silent Spring,* which sounded the first alarm about the fatal threat to animal life posed by the pesticide DDT. "Both women," Docherty writes, "regard nature with an unabashed sense of wonder and bring aesthetic sensibility to bear on its defense." In the current show, both *Pygmy Pond Lily,* and *Late Winter Birds* pop out of their boxes like gifts of beauty to the world. Their fragile presences compel our attention.

Another artist whose work bears comparison with Carson's is **Kate Cheney Chappell.** In fact, Carson has been "a guiding light in my life," Chappell says. For a recent show in honor of the fiftieth anniversary of the publication of *Silent Spring,* Chappell created a series of prints and watercolors of birds, nests and eggs, starfish and sea urchins in tide pools and among the rocks of Monhegan Island, where she summers. "The more I draw," Chappell writes, "the more I see." But though the life of the earth is celebrated in Chappell's work, she is also aware of the possibility of loss. In *Requiem,* for example, a blood red sun is orbited by a seemingly dead planet in a black sky over a tombstone-shaped form standing in the midst of falling leaves and spiked with porcupine quills and bamboo tines.

Judy Allen-Efstanthiou, *The Tree Museum: American Chestnut Blight with Subtitles* (detail)

Goodale and Chappell offer hope that it is not too late for warnings to be heeded; **Judith Allen-Efstathiou** in her series *Tree Museum* is less sanguine. This work documents irredeemable loss: the American chestnut, decimated in Appalachia in the 1920s by blight; the immense elms of Portland, destroyed in the 1950s and 60s by disease; and currently the Ottoman-era date palms of Athens, dying in unprecedented numbers from a Middle-Eastern red beetle infestation. Allen-Efstathiou has an emotional relationship with all these trees. Her father was born in Appalachia; the loss of the American chestnut forced his family to change their entire way of life. Her mother is a Maine native and Allen-Efstathiou remembers as a child seeing the tree-lined avenues of the city, now gone forever. She herself lives half the year in Greece, and is now seeing and through her art bearing witness to the loss of the city's magnificent date palms. In *Tree Museum*, a work that memorializes what has been lost, the extinct chestnut appears as a negative, as though all that remains is a trace, like an x-ray, a ghostly image, while the elm seems to be its own ghost, composed of layered shadows of itself.

Care for the earth can also reveal itself in the materials an artist chooses to work with. **Melita Westerlund** works in steel, aluminum, and more recently recycled fiber. She uses painted aluminum strips in work such as *Silent Flow* and *Bouquet*, whose colorful metallic flowers play ironically with our expectations of the idea of bouquet. *In Sea Meadow*, Westerlund fills the gallery space with a virtual meadow of colorful sculptures made of recycled fiber representing endangered coral. It is a work in which the artist not only raises our consciousness about a threat to a form of life, but at the same time, in her use of material, demonstrates how each of us in our lives and work can do something to protect and preserve our world.

"Who," **Marlene Gerberick** asks

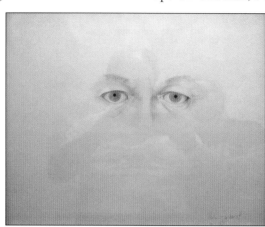

Marlene Gerberick, *Clarence*

when describing her work, "can look up and out into the heavens on a dark night and not react in awe?" Finding meaning in this sense of awe is the motivating force in Gerberick's work. Her collages of found objects counterpoise the natural and the man-made: a fork, a glass shard, an iron spike wrapped in rope on one side, a single leaf, a twig on the other. Her drawings and images are magical and mysterious: a dark horse stands in the gallery in front of four white arms with hands upraised and a wooden box carrying a glass bulb. Through objects found in forests, stones and animal bones, remnants of the living world, and from fragments found amidst the discards of human life, remnants of human history, Gerberick creates a visual poetry, dark and dream-like, contemplative and reflective.

Barbara Goodbody is an artist/traveler who sees her work as "an art of stewardship." She first travelled to India in 1986, where she began what was to become a decades-long project of photographing village life and sacred sites on the subcontinent. Journeying around the world with her camera, she has consistently captured images of life as it is lived and environments in which human beings and nature interact.

JUDITH ALLEN-EFSTANTHIOU

In my recent work I explore artists as archivist and botanist, recording loss in the natural world caused by human activities. Far from "scientific" this work highlights the partial, fragmentary, and highly subjective nature of the research. Documentation here functions not so much as a recording for posterity but as an act of mourning. In a series of large lithographs of blighted trees, with smaller *Footnote* drawings and prints, I develop narratives out of a need to memorialize the trees documented.

The Tree Museum: Elm Tree Blight with Subtitles, 2011,
paper lithograph on 4 layers of mulberry paper, 36" x 48".

My goal as an artist is to be, in poet Mary Oliver's words, "a bride married to amazement." It begins with attention to the interdependence of all life on this planet, noticing the "li", dynamic patterns across many forms. Breathing in, breathing out, we depend on the environment, yet we act as if we are above it all, indifferent to our agency in its pollution. Rachel Carson warned us 50 years ago that if we poison the land, we poison ourselves. I create art that confronts harm to the fragile web of life and speaks to an ethos of care.

PHOTOGRAPH BY MICHAEL BOUCHER

Medusa/Starfish I, 2012, collagraph, 26" x 19".

A deep need to understand the incredible gift of life, my work has long incorporated elements of all that surrounds us, whether of the natural world or of human creation.

Who can look up and out into the heavens on a dark night and not react in awe?

I've responded most fully (in my quest) to the forests of the northern regions. As well, I've found fragments of possibilities in old, dust filled bulk stores. (Ideas whispered through fragments of a page.) This has been especially true in Finland and Iceland.

I am in the studio daily because that is my way and place to examine life. My work has been and is a quest to find answers which can only be identified as a feeling in the deep inner being . . . the ah ha! of intuition and insight. The search for meaning. The unending search.

PHOTOGRAPH BY RAY MICHAUD

Language Vessel, 1996, mixed media, 14" x 11".

My photographic journey has been lifelong, using light and shadow always in search of inner presence. My most intense photographic experiences were the years I spent delving into the actual sites of the Holocaust period of history. Seeing, feeling and recording man's capacity for evil was life-changing. My images are meaningful to me. They all tell a story.

Execution Wall, Auschwitz Concentration Camp, Poland, 1988, gelatin silver print, 19.25" x 13.25".
Courtesy Howard Greenberg Gallery.

REBECCA GOODALE

On January 1, 2000 I began a new body of work that has taken shape as a series of artist's books about the plants and animals currently listed as threatened or endangered by the State of Maine. At this time there are more than 200 plants listed and nearly 50 animals. My intention is not to become a scientific illustrator; instead I want to inspire sensitivity for these rare species by using my background in book arts and textile design to interpret what I see with color, pattern, rhythm, and transition.

Pygmy Water-lily, 2012, open artist's book: screen prints with paste paper, 30" x 28" x 5".

My photographs are a representation of my work since 1986 when I began photographing village life, sacred sites, and cultures with a focus on India.

My latest work has been referencing the world and the power of connection and commonality we, as human beings, have with our environment and life on Earth.

And Dream with the Dreaming Earth We Will, 2012, photograph, 17" x 22".

We need artists to help explain what is happening in this country, to tell the truth and reveal the lies, to be willing to say the emperor has no clothes, to create moral indignation, to envision alternatives, to reinvent language. We need artists to help us come together and share our voices and build community around powerful issues concerning our roles in the world and our planet's survival. Compassion must be translated into action.

(Natasha's words on portrait painted by Robert Shetterly for *Americans Who Tell the Truth* series.)

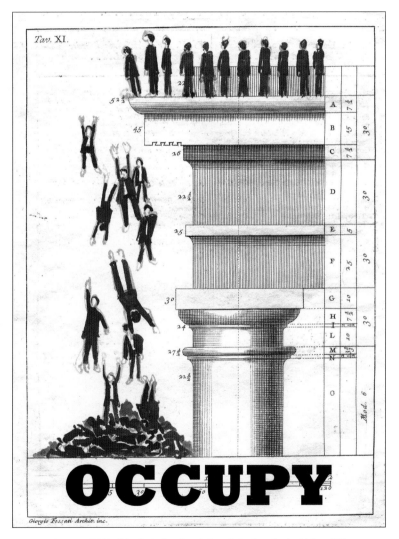

Occupy, 2011–12, digital print (of an ink drawing), 11" x 17".

Events in my life have been the inspiration for my artwork. Childhood trauma damaged my connection to my body and my life's work has been to regain that connection. A deep relationship with Nature established the spiritual grounding for my creative expression.

My early work involved earth and landscape imagery. Then in the late 1990s, in conjunction with my own healing, I began using my body in art making. By combining the figure with Nature, I experienced healing and transformation. I then shared these celebrations of the body with others. Facilitating healing using art has not only changed my life but has also become my spiritual path as I support others to do the same.

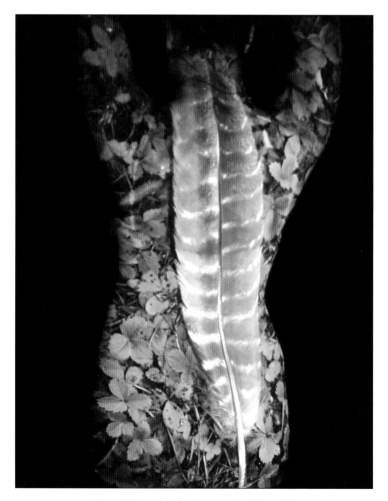

Digi, 2008, archival photograph, 25" x 21".

I'm not a political painter who wants to persuade people with my images. I'm more interested in preserving a record of the time and of how it felt to be alive in this time. Sometimes I start a painting with a clear intention to paint about a particular event. Sometimes my concerns sneak into my paintings by the back door. In either case, I have no idea how these concerns will express themselves, nor of how the painting will finally look.

Three in One, 2001, tempera on paper, 30" x 40".

My work is based on the attributes and narratives of traditional textiles. I am interested in the dynamics of pattern: how pattern orders the natural world, how it gathers and transmits evidence of passing time. My paintings reference textiles that enhance shelter and identify the human body. My current work is based on the traditional practice of piecing garments and domestic furnishings from scraps of cloth that exist in many cultures around the world.

PHOTOGRAPH BY JAY YORK

Kasaya I, 2012, collage with hand printed paper on wood, 40" x 54".
Courtesy Aucocisco Galleries, Portland, Maine.

MELITA WESTERLUND

Over many years I have been exploring the interrelationship of color and form. The shapes and colors have been inspired by a combination of my American and African experiences and my traditional Finnish background. I have continuously chosen to work in a variety of mediums. My current sculpture consists of explorations with aluminum, both polished and polychromed, and cotton fiber, continuing my coral series.

Koralli Saari, Blue, 2010, cotton fiber, pigment, wire mesh, 30" x 31"x 15".

EXPANDING THE CREATIVE FRONTIER

Jessica Skwire Routhier

". . . as the Polar Star has been considered the mariner's guide and director in conducting the ship over the pathless ocean to the desired haven, and as the center of magnetic attraction; as it has been figuratively used to denote the point, to which all affections turn, and as it is here intended to represent the State, it may be considered the citizens' guide, and the object to which the patriot's best exertions should be directed."

—First session of the
Maine State Legislature, 1820

What does it mean to be a leader? This section of the *Maine Women Pioneers III* exhibition—named after Maine's state motto, *Dirigo*, Latin for "I Lead"—attempts to grapple with that question. Worded another way, what does it mean to be a "Woman Pioneer" in the arts? For after all, "leading" is the distinguishing characteristic of a pioneer, defined variously as "one who ventures into unknown territory" or "one who opens up new areas of thought, research, or development." Is a Maine Woman Pioneer in the Arts like the North Star that is pictured on the Great Seal of the State of Maine: a sort of celebrity compass, visible and accessible to all, a "point to which all affections turn?" Or is she like the sailor, pulling inspiration from the state's tide of creativity? Perhaps she is like the farmer with his scythe, patiently nurturing and then reaping the fruits of her endeavors, or she could be like the pine tree, seemingly limitless in her capacity to renew herself and provide for others.

Then again, historically, we're more inclined to view the great artist as something like the solitary and stalwart moose, forging its own way and casting a wide shadow in its path. Indeed, the eighteen artists represented here do loom large in the Maine art scene. They have taught, organized, provoked, innovated, published, and traveled, constantly expanding the boundaries of creative discourse in Maine. Their own art is their frontier, that object to which their best exertions are directed, both inside and outside of the geographical and cultural map of Maine.

Of course, women pioneers have always

had to do more than just settle the wilderness. Art historians like Linda Nochlin and Griselda Pollock have long observed that women artists have had to stake their claim in the art scene to a degree that men have not. For centuries, restrictions on female behavior meant that

Josefina Auslender, *Difuso*

formal artistic study was possible only under unusual circumstances; later, women and girls in art classes were often challenged by institutionalized, sometimes unconscious biases that directed them toward more domestic or commercial outlets for their talents. Even among those who stormed the fine arts scene, there was often a tacit understanding that the most aggressively avant-garde movements of the twentieth century remained the domain of men.

Artists like **Josefina Auslender**, **Noriko Sakanishi**, and **Diane Bowie Zaitlin** have challenged that perception for the last two decades and beyond. Zaitlin's gestural encaustic-and-collage paintings compel the viewer to grapple with materials, surfaces, and technique as forcibly as any Abstract Expressionist work of the postwar era, and Auslender and Sakanishi's architectural, geometric abstractions interpret for a new generation the muscular Minimalism of

the 1960s and '70s. In Sakanishi's words, "I believe I have, in a sense, led by example as a woman artist working in the area of abstract art. There were very few of us in Maine when I came out of MECA [the Maine College of Art, then the Portland School of Art] in the early 1970s." Auslender also worked against marginalization politically in her native Argentina, where artists and intellectuals were objects of suspicion during the dictatorial regimes of the 1970s and '80s (she immigrated to Maine in the late 1980s). For their part, Zaitlin and Sakanishi have found that their abstract idioms provide a way to engage disabled students, also so often disenfranchised in the worlds of art and politics.

These artists came of age during an era when feminist art, feminist art history, and art by women were practically synonymous concepts. Groundbreaking treatises like Pollock's *Why Have There Been No Great Women Artists?* (1971) teased out an array of answers to that fundamental question, including the observation that women and their bodies have historically been *subjects* for art rather than its auteurs. Theorist Linda Nochlin cheekily turned the tables with her provocative photograph *Buy My Bananas*—published in Norma Broude and Mary D. Gerrard's *The Power of Feminist Art* (1972)—a gender-bending and decidedly phallic subversion of a nineteenth-century image of a *demimondaine* with her nude breasts tantalizingly propped up on a tray of luscious-looking apples.

The point of Nochlin's photo was to expose the absurdity of this sexualized gaze when the image-maker is female and the subject male, and for 1972, she made a pretty strong case. However, the last forty years have seen great evolution both in women's art and in gender studies. It seems less strange, now, to see **Denise Froehlich**'s frankly sensual, large-format, digital photographs of nude male torsos and pelvises, or **Melonie Bennett**'s reconceptualized Madonna and Child (note the cross motifs) in her reverential *Tyler's First Day Home*, in which the father and baby's plump physiques and tonsured pates pleasingly resemble each other. The figures in Bennett's photo inhabit a resolutely male world of wood paneling, motorcycle posters, and sectional sofas; her exploration of it is almost anthropological, as one might respectfully approach a foreign shrine. The male world is also a subject of **Katherine Bradford**'s paintings, which deflate myths of patriarchy by positing, for example, an image of two men kissing as an illustration for

Katherine Cobey, *Danger Dress*

the word "MEN," or by showing a pantsless, footless Superman who appears to be washing his "S" badge by the riverbank. Bradford's beleaguered superhero recalls Nochlin's banana-seller, though he is rendered a bit more sympathetically.

Mary Hart and **Elizabeth Cashin McMillan** also explore bodies in their work, though only parts of bodies. The grasping, fumbling fingers and scattered eyes of McMillan's work suggest a dissembled version of that art-historical "gaze," a visual interpretation, perhaps, of the parental admonition to "look with your eyes and not with your hands." Mary Hart's *Gulch* presents a desiccated animal spine and pelvis within a desert-like landscape. "I seek to draw the viewer close," writes Hart, "to create a direct emotional experience of the sensual quality inherent in natural objects." The intimate close-up of this flesh-colored ravine, bisected by bone, suggests female physicality in a way that is reminiscent of that "Great Woman Artist" Georgia O'Keeffe.

The nature of femininity and the femininity of nature remain topics of interest for Maine women in the arts. **Allison Cooke Brown** and **Katherine Cobey** use traditional female textile arts to explore issues of adornment, protection, vulnerability, and aging. Textiles are also a point of departure for **Grace DeGennaro**'s patterned paintings inspired by nineteenth-century Navajo weavings. "As always," DeGennaro writes, "ritual, growth and the passage of time are the themes." Female creativity and self-adornment as foundations of community are also subjects of **Barbara Sullivan**'s witty fresco *Beauty Shop*. It seems notable that the women's plaster torsos are jaggedly bisected, while their elaborate rolled coiffures are fully intact and visible through transparent hooded dryers.

Barbara Sullivan, *Running Late*

Sullivan's *Bird Guide*, with its beplumed, chattering denizens, offers a parallel in the animal world. The impossible variety of birds—each an individual shaped fresco affixed to a stand of trees articulated with black Sharpie—recalls the *Peaceable Kingdom* motif of nineteenth-century American art, a pantheistic world in which unlikely animal companions coexist in nature. **Susan Amons** also uses distinctive materials to delve into the animal world. Her unique form of monumental printmaking, using layered Mylar cut-outs, produces images of waterfowl and other wildlife that are, in her words, "multiple and varied, brilliantly frontal, or receding in space like the animals themselves, a memory, mysterious, and wild by nature."

Janice Kasper explores a related idea in her *Shadow Species* series, in which richly colored silhouettes of vanishing Maine species—wolves, bears, frogs—are seen through intricate screens of twigs and leaves. Kasper, who has held artist residencies at two national parks, focuses on environmental concerns in both her personal and artistic life. As she writes, her work "has consistently been concerned with growing development in New England and especially to the effect of sprawl on our wildlife populations.... I hope to make the viewer aware of these changes before permanent harm is done."

Maine has a long tradition of environmental activism, from public figures like Rachel Carson and Edmund Muskie to the quieter, grassroots efforts of back-to-the-landers. **Keliy Anderson-Staley** pulls on the cords connecting Maine politics and nature in her photographic series entitled *Off the Grid*. In these frank color images, Anderson-Staley captures the homes and daily lives of thirty Maine families who have chosen to live unconnected to an electrical grid, a community in which she herself was raised. "I do not want to over-romanticize this way of living or over-estimate the role it might play in resolving the global environmental crisis," she writes, and indeed her photos are candid, unvarnished and detached. Still, the hand-made, vernacular quality of the homes depicted is undeniably alluring, with the octagonal form of one building strongly echoing the architecture of Revolutionary War forts. **Dozier Bell**, with her painting *Barbican*, also depicts a defensive structure and seems similarly motivated by concerns about humankind's lasting imprint upon the world. The shadowy, ruined battlement seems to exist in a post-apocalyptic landscape, begging the question: What was being defended? And is it still there?

Like all human constructions, art, too, is transient. **Meggan Gould**'s photographs of blackboards, computer desktops, and the back sides of snapshots show, to some degree, what is left behind after the creating is done. **Celeste Roberge** also explores impermanence and futility with her fragile seaweed boats, so delicate as to be transparent, and surely incapable of entering the water without returning immediately to their amorphous, osmotic state. Particularly for an artist like Roberge, who has created permanent, commissioned sculptures for collections from Maine to California, there is an irony in creating art that can so readily un-create itself. The irony is extended in the more solid, bronze versions of these seaweed boats,

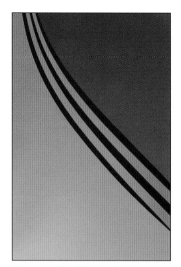

Meggan Gould, *Don't Open Box in the Light #14*

which Roberge has pierced with holes so that they, too, can neither hold anything nor float.

Roberge's oarless boats, with their pronounced bowsprits, are timeless and iconic in appearance. They recall the boat in Thomas Cole's famous *Voyage of Life* series from 1842, which carries its passenger through a series of landscapes representing the stages of life. Throughout the four paintings, the passenger receives guidance from an angelic figure—his own North Star or "mariner's guide and director"—but he makes the journey resolutely on his own in his frail little vessel.

Maine's women pioneers in the arts have similarly braved the currents of the state's cultural landscape, holding up a lantern to others who follow in their wake. They lead, more than anything else, by breaking ground in their own artistic pursuits and expanding the creative frontier so that there is always more to explore. They are laborers, leaders, trailblazers: they are pioneers.

• • •

JESSICA SKWIRE ROUTHIER is the current President of Maine Archives and Museums. She is a free-lance editor, writer, and an independent museum professional who lives in South Portland.

In winter, I work on large-scale prints inspired by images that I record from nature throughout the year. I create a group of Mylar shapes which I ink, print, and re-ink; building up color layers and altering spatial relationships. A series of related work evolves from the printed collection of cut out shapes. What I enjoy most about this process is that I am able to pursue multiple variations of my original idea. The final prints are multiple and varied, brilliantly frontal, or receding in space like the animals themselves, a memory, mysterious, and wild by nature.

Red Tailed Hawks I, 2011, monotype with pastel, 33" x 44".

Off the Grid documents thirty families who have chosen to live in Maine disconnected from the electrical grid. I am especially interested in depicting the relationships between people and their homes. I grew up in one of these cabins, and this project started with my family. Returning to photograph where I grew up, I was aware of being both an insider and an outsider. It is important to engage in discussions about how our domestic lives impact the broader world, but I do not want to over-romanticize this way of living or over-estimate the role it might play in resolving the global environmental crisis.

Hanson's Tent at Common Ground Fair, Unity, Maine, 2008, C-Print, edition: 1 of 5, framed in blonde wood with plexiglass, no mat, 20" x 24".

What I'd like to do is to present people with a range of abstract images and give them the chance to see what they are most able to discover in it, wringing out, little by little, all of the feelings of aesthetic beauty and drama that life contains. These possibilities make the work ever-living and ever-changing at the very instant someone is looking at it. In time, this same reality returns as a work of art in the form of light, shadows, volumes, color.

PHOTOGRAPH BY JAY YORK

Voyage, graphite and colored pencil on paper, 14" x 19.5", 2010.

A few themes persist in all my work: the past as it exists in the present; the cyclical nature of catastrophic events as part of the continuity of human experience; the transformation of experience through the processes of memory; and the primacy of animal consciousness (by which I mean the consciousness we share with animals, birds, and insects).

Barbican, 2010, charcoal on Mylar, 3.25" x 4".
Courtesy Aucocisco Galleries, Portland, Maine; Danese Gallery, New York, New York.

I like to photograph real life and real people. I continue the ongoing visual diary of my family and friends in their various everyday life situations, which sometimes seem not so everyday. I love to point things out that I can't believe are happening in front of me and share them with others. This naturally led me to photographing in public venues in much the same way, hoping to capture relationships and interactions between people that I do not know.

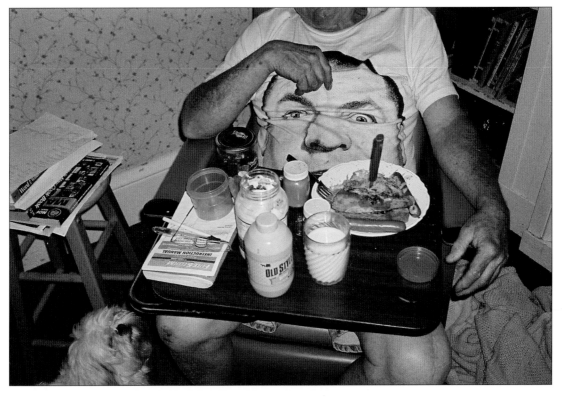

Dad's Dinner, 2011, gelatin silver print, 13.5" x 19.5".

The four paintings that I am submitting have either the word "MEN" in them or show images of men. One shows two men kissing; another shows two men waiting to vacuum; a third shows a Superman separated from his insignia; and the forth and largest painting shows the words "NEW MEN" painted within an abstract border. The words "NEW MEN" can be seen as a call for males to become new, to transform themselves. On the other hand, the words "NEW MEN" can also be taken as declarative and celebratory. A few months ago the art critic John Yau called my latest work "meditations on masculinity."

Men, 2011, oil on canvas, 12" x 9". Collection of Ed Hauser.

My work ranges from small hand held book-like structures to larger scale sculpture. I am attracted to linens and women's clothing as a materials source; traditionally female activities such as sewing or knitting; and domesticity/female issues as subject matter. I constantly wrestle with what I feel society has proscribed as the ideal feminine behavior of being a compliant "good girl" versus my personal need to "act out," to become my own person.

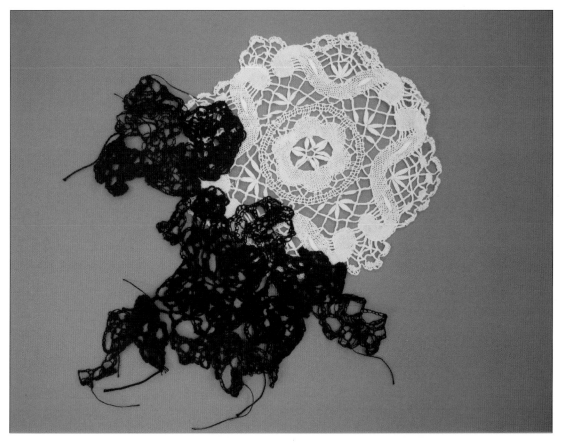

Amended (#11), 2012, crochet doily, cotton thread, 11.5" x 12".

I started out knitting clothing; I have ended up seeing knitting as a sculptural tool, and clothing as evocative off the body as on it. I spin wool and silk, cotton and flax. I make other yarns from plastic bags, telephone wire, and kitchen "chore boys." In an installation, the armatures, the position of the figures, the drape, everything matters.

PHOTOGRAPH BY DAVID B. COBEY

Portrait of Alzheimer's, 1992, hand spun silk and woolen shawl hung on wooden clothes hanger suspended from ceiling by monofilament over glass base, 77" x 28", elevated on 4 plastic tubes, 8" high, diameter 4".

Archetypal forms and their ability to communicate ideas that transcend both language and culture is the subject of my work. My studio practice is one of identifying resonant images that are both iconic and numinous. This vocabulary of geometric images includes: concentric circles, diamonds, crosses and the *vesica piscis* shape.

On an inviolable ground, the paintings are rendered through a deliberate accretion of dots, beads and transparent glazes of color. The accumulation of marks and glazes of color reflects and supports the recurrent themes of ritual, growth, memory and the passage of time.

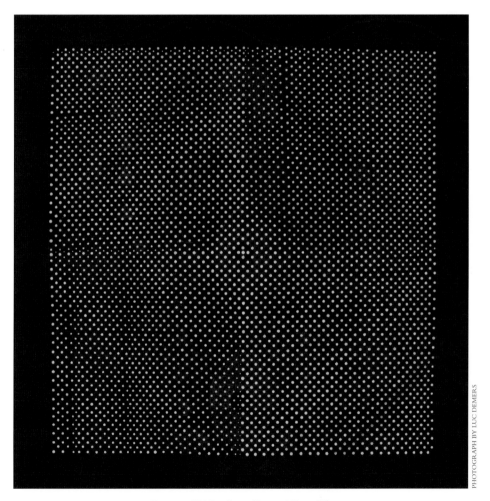

PHOTOGRAPH BY LUC DEMERS

Dreams, 2012, oil on linen, 40" x 40".
Courtesy Aucocisco Galleries, Portland, Maine.

My image making often starts with a book. I began reading Roland Barthes' *A Lover's Discourse: Fragments* and I was thinking about past lovers, partnerships and attractions and also about how our perception of these things change as we age.

I decided to photograph the men I know over the age of 40. The work you see comes from an ongoing series and leaves an impression of the male body that reflects my thoughts on virility, ageing, beauty and the opposite sex. They were made with a Holga and 3200 speed film. The negatives were then scanned and printed on a large-scale inkjet printer.

Shades of Love and Suffering (from the Pathos of Eros series), 2012,
ink jet print from a digital negative, 47" x 72" x 4".

Considerations of vision—of how we look at the world at large, as well as how we customarily employ photography to document and speak to our surroundings—have long been central to my interests within photography. What do we look at photographically, and what do we ignore? I continually explore these ideas visually, most recently via examinations of the backs of photographs, the mediation of the camera's viewfinder, blackboards, and computer screens.

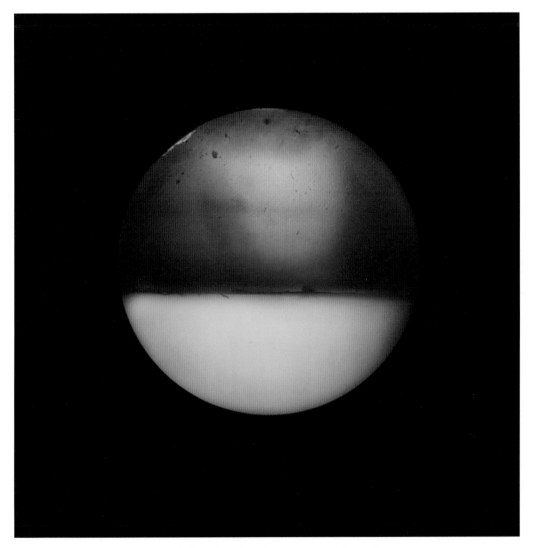

Viewfinder #37, 2012, pigment print, 16" x 16".

MARY HART

The compositions in my paintings are very simple and their size is intimate. I seek to draw the viewer close, to create a direct emotional experience of the sensual quality inherent in natural objects. I think of my paintings as short poems, connecting childhood memory with adult concerns.

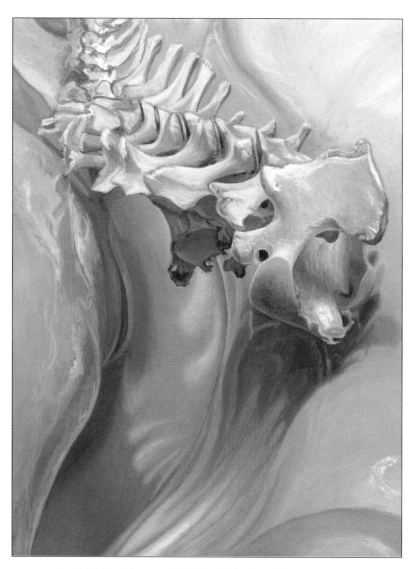

Gulch, 2006, oil on panel, 3⅞" x 3" (unframed); 16.5" x 15".
Courtesy Aucocisco Galleries, Portland, Maine.

JANICE KASPER

My work has consistently been concerned with growing development in New England and especially to the effect of sprawl on our wildlife populations. I moved to Maine from Connecticut in 1974 where I have seen open spaces and forestlands divided and developed. Through my work I hope to make the viewer aware of these changes before permanent harm is done. I am trying to resist being dictatorial so my work is often tempered with humor. I also keep forward in my mind that although the message is important, the work should firstly be read as an artfully painted surface.

Ghosts, 2009, oil on board, 24" x 24".
Courtesy Caldbeck Gallery, Rockland, Maine.

PHOTOGRAPH BY BOB BROOKS

In 2010 I was challenged to show a series of small paintings. I wanted to paint only larger paintings and this decision influenced a group of paintings I called the *Compression Series*. Each painting was a small space I linked to a larger space in my mind. I thought about what it would be like in color field space occupied with a very small concentrated task and partial view. In the end, this expanded from points of view into a whole. After completing the series, I realized that I had begun to feel like some people say they feel when they look at my larger paintings.

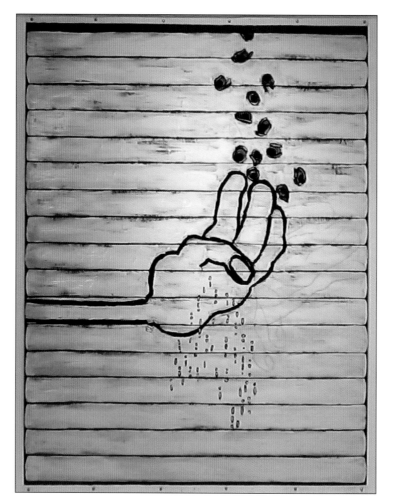

Untitled, 2009, oil on paper, 36" x 47".
Courtesy Aucocisco Gallery, Portland, Maine.

Although sea lace is intriguing and beautiful in form and material, at first I could not think what I would do to transform it into a sculpture. After observing gatherers of seaweed along the Nova Scotia shores in their flat-bottomed boats laden with rockweed, I thought, "Why not a boat, a seaweed boat, better yet, a seaweed boat that cannot float."

Sealace Boat, 2012, Sealace (Latin: agarum cribosum), 4.5" x 12" x 6".

From being a college student to becoming a professional artist, I have lived and worked in Maine virtually all of my adult life. I have previously said that my art, which combines sculpture and painting, comes from a mysterious, intuitive place within me. But I am sure it would not be as strong as I want it to be if I had not found a unique source of creative energy and artistic courage in this inspiring place.

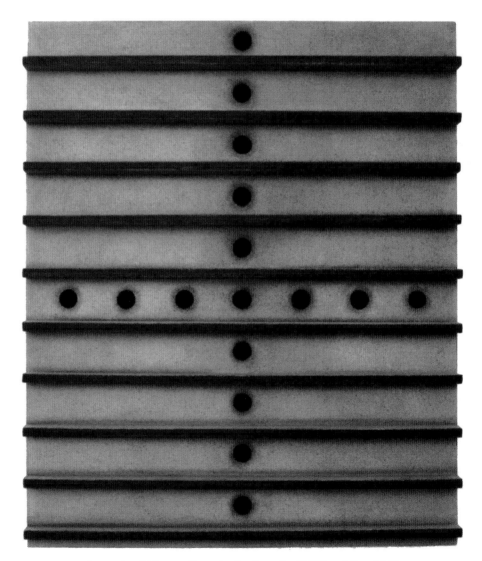

Intersection, 2006, acrylic and mixed media, 30.75" x 26" x 5.25".
Courtesy June Fitzpatrick Gallery, Portland, Maine.

The "EVERYDAY" fresco objects and installations that I make tell stories. Especially about everyday places where we all have spent time; the commonality of our known and similar everyday experiences connect us with one another. As I present the familiar over and over again, it is my hope that my audience will act as voyeurs eavesdropping with humor and irony back on themselves.

PHOTOGRAPH BY JAY YORK

Bird Guide, 2012, sharpie drawing with shaped fresco attached, 76" x 72" x 6".
Courtesy Caldbeck Gallery, Rockland, Maine.

I have always been attracted to worn and distressed surfaces in my surroundings. I love the rich patinas created in nature and over time from man; rusty discarded items, old tools that show the hand of the user, old documents with fine calligraphy, peeling paint. All are surfaces with a history of their own. This is a sense that I work for in my paintings through layers of color, texture, words and images. The paintings have suggestions of memory, bits of conversation, or perhaps a sense of a person, location or period of time.

Multiple Choice A, 2010, mixed media encaustic, 24" x 24".

PHOTOGRAPH BY GARY LOWELL

ARTIST BIOGRAPHIES

VANGUARD

SUSAN BICKFORD [1963]

NEWCASTLE, MAINE

For the past ten years Bickford's choice of media has been projected video/animation/sound for interactive installation and theater. In January 2012 Susan collaborated with three artists to create *FLOAT/PLAY*, an immersive interactive installation in the Charles Danforth Galley at UMA. She has designed projections for numerous productions including *Metamorphoses* at Colby College and *Sunday in the Park with George* at Heartwood Regional Theater Company. In September 2009 she installed *Precarious Balance*, a solo show of interactive video installation, electronic sculpture, drawing and collaborative performance at the Danforth Galley at UMA. *FF: Duet for Piano, Hydraulic Lift and Volume F* was performed at the Portland Museum of Art in 2006. With roots seven generations deep in Maine, Bickford lives with her partner Rich Simon and daughter Bella.

DIANA CHERBULIEZ [1965]

VINALHAVEN, MAINE

"I have always looked through analytic and metaphoric lenses. My parents—a psychiatrist, a landscape architect, and beekeepers—sensitized me to the systems that guide and structure our perceptions, whether aesthetic, theoretical, structural, man-made, or organic. Art school exposed me to comprehensive history and theory, gave me problem solving skills and bravado, while my technical abilities developed as an artist's assistant, in a special effects shop, and on renovation and restoration projects. My location and situation provide sculptural material and influence the aesthetics and rhythm of my work. Self-conscious and post-modern, like my sculpture, I, too, am a product of my makers' intellect and environment."

AMY STACEY CURTIS [1970]

LYMAN, MAINE

In 1998, Amy Stacey Curtis began what would be an 18-year commitment to art-making, a project culminating through 9 solo-biennial exhibits from 2000 to 2016. In the end, Curtis will have installed 81 large-in-scope, interactive installation and new-media works in the vast mills of 8 or 9 Maine, USA towns. Each solo-biennial exhibit is a 22-month process, each exhibit exploring a different theme while requiring audiences to perpetuate its multiple installations. The recipient of the Maine Arts Commission's 2005 Individual Artist Fellowship for Visual Art and five Good Idea Grants, Curtis has committed to this work to convey that we are a part of a whole, that everyone and everything is connected and affects.

ALICIA EGGERT [1981]

PORTLAND, MAINE

Alicia Eggert earned a bachelor's degree in Interior Design from Drexel University in Philadelphia, studied Scandinavian architecture and design in Denmark, and worked at an architectural firm in New York for several years before pursuing a career in art. She received an MFA in Sculpture/ Dimensional Studies from Alfred University in 2009. Since then, her work has been shown at the Triennale Design Museum in Milan, SIGGRAPH Asia in Hong Kong, the Portland Museum of Art in Maine, the Everson Museum of Art in Syracuse, and at institutions in Canada, New York, Philadelphia, Boston, Seattle, St. Louis and elsewhere. Later this year, her work will be featured in the International Symposium on Electronic Art (ISEA2012) at the Albuquerque Museum of Art and History, the

16th Annual Sculpture by the Sea exhibition in Sydney, Australia, the Art Moves Festival in Torun, Poland, and Cyberfest in St. Petersburg, Russia. She currently is an Assistant Professor of Art at Bowdoin College.

LAUREN FENSTERSTOCK [1975]
PORTLAND, MAINE

Lauren Fensterstock is an artist, writer, and curator based in Portland, Maine. Lauren's work is held in private and public collections in the US, Europe and Asia. Her artwork has been featured in recent exhibitions at the Austin Museum of Art (TX), the Bowdoin College Museum of Art (ME), the San Francisco Museum of Craft and Design (CA), the Jordan Schnitzer Museum of Art (OR), the DUMBO Art Center (NY), the Dorsky Gallery (NY), and the Oliver Sears Gallery (Ireland). Her work will be the subject of a major solo exhibition at the John Michael Kohler Art Center (WI) in February 2013.

Outside the studio, Lauren recently served as the Academic Program Director of the MFA in Studio Arts at Maine College of Art and as Director of the Institute of Contemporary Art at Maine College of Art. Her curatorial projects and published writings have been featured internationally. Lauren holds degrees from the Parsons School of Design (BFA 1997) and SUNY, New Paltz (MFA 2000). She is represented by Aucocisco Galleries.

LIHUA LEI [1966]
SOLON, MAINE

Lihua Lei was a participant at Skowhegan School of Painting and Sculpture in 1998. Lei's work blurs the distinction between installation, performance and sculpture. As a child she observed her older brothers sculpt roosters, pigs and goats from rice flour dough as part of Taoist rituals performed annually at her family's chicken coops and barns to express their appreciation for the harvest nature provides. Her cultural sensibility has enhanced her ability to engage the viewer through both traditional and unconventional media. Gratitude and reverence for all life, and her unwavering view of human beings as noble continue to be major themes in her thinking and her art.

JULIE POITRAS SANTOS [1967]
PORTLAND, MAINE

Julie Poitras Santos' solo and collaborative work has been exhibited internationally at the Museum of Contemporary Art in Denver, the Reykjanesbaer Art Museum in Iceland and at the Centre for Contemporary Culture in Barcelona, Spain, among others. She has attended residencies and created performances and projects in Vermont, Spain, France, Germany, the Netherlands and Iceland. A new piece investigating textile and narrative was exhibited at Coleman Burke Gallery in Brunswick, Maine earlier this year in *A Thickening Rhythm*, a group exhibition she curated. Poitras Santos is on the core faculty of the Maine College of Art MFA Program in Studio Arts.

CARRIE SCANGA [1977]
PORTLAND, MAINE

Carrie Scanga's etchings, drawings, and sculptural installations have been exhibited internationally at venues including the International Print Center, New York, the Janet Turner Print Museum, Chico, CA, the EKWC in the Netherlands, and El Conteiner in Quito, Ecuador. Numerous awards have supported the development of her work, including two consecutive winter fellowships from the Fine Arts Work Center in Provincetown, a fellowship from the New York Foundation for the Arts, residencies at The MacDowell Colony, the Blue Mountain Center, Fundación Valparaíso, Sculpture Space, Artspace, and the Salina Art Center, and grants from the Pollock Krasner Foundation and the Ludwig Vogelstein Foundation. Scanga is an art professor at Bowdoin College.

LING-WEN TSAI [1970]
PORTLAND, MAINE

Ling-Wen Tsai was born in Tainan, Taiwan. Tsai's practice spans a broad range of media, and her work has taken the form of installation, performance, video, photography, painting, drawing and combinations of these media. In 2003, Tsai was awarded an Artist Residency at the Cité Internationale des Arts, Paris, France. Her work has been exhibited internationally and nationally: Paris, France; Tainan, Taiwan; Baghdad, Iraq; New York; Chicago, IL; Boston, MA; Siena, Italy; Berlin, Germany. Tsai is a Professor of Sculpture and New Media, and is currently Chair of the Sculpture Department at Maine College of Art.

• • •

LOIS DODD [1927]
CUSHING, MAINE & BROOKLYN, NEW YORK

Lois Dodd was born in Montclair, NJ in 1927. From 1945 to1948 she attended The Cooper Union in New York. By 1952, she was a key member of New York's postwar art scene and became a founding member of one of the 10th Street cooperatives, Tanager Gallery, working beside Charles Cajori, Philip Pearlstein, William King, Alex Katz, and others; she exhibited there until 1962. It was after finding a second home in Maine in the early '50s that Dodd embarked on her journey into direct observation and landscape painting. Dodd taught at Brooklyn College and, since 1980, served on the Board of Governors of the Skowhegan School of Painting and Sculpture. She is an elected member of the American Academy and Institute of Arts and Letters and the National Academy of Design. She is represented by the Alexandre Gallery in New York and the Caldbeck Gallery in Rockland, Maine.

MAGGIE FOSKETT [1919]
CAMDEN, MAINE & SANIBEL, FLORIDA

Maggie Foskett grew up in Brazil and graduated from Bryn Mawr College. She did not become seriously interested in photography until, at age 57, she took a workshop with Ansel Adams. In 1995 she stopped using a camera or negative and makes her own glass plates composed from fragments of vegetation. Foskett also prints from x-rays of injured wildlife to suggest the vulnerability of their shrinking habitat. Solo exhibitions of Foskett's work have been shown at the Farnsworth Museum and the Center for Maine Contemporary Art, ME, the Evansville Museum of Arts and Sciences, IN, Bryn Mawr College, PA, and the National Academy of Sciences, Washington, DC.

SUSAN GROCE [1954]

MARTINSVILLE, MAINE

Susan Groce received her MFA from the University of Michigan. She has worked at Atelier 17, Paris; the Edinburgh Printmakers, Scotland; Open Bite Print Workshop, Australia and the MacDowell Colony, NH. She has been an Artist in Residence, Visiting Artist, Guest Lecturer and Visiting Researcher (safer print practices) at over 40 art schools, print workshops and universities in Australia, Ireland, Northern Ireland, England, Scotland, Canada, and the USA. Susan is currently a Professor of Art at the University of Maine. Her prints and drawings have been in over 180 solo, invitational and juried exhibitions and are included in private, public and corporate collections in the USA, Portugal, Argentina, the UK, Australia, New Zealand, South Africa, Singapore and Canada.

BEVERLY HALLAM [1923]

YORK, MAINE

"I had very academic training at the Massachusetts School of Art. After graduating, I painted in a very realistic way using oil and a variety of subject matter. In the early 50s, I began using polyvinyl acetate, now called acrylic, and my work gradually became semi-realistic, almost abstract. From the 60s to the 80s I concentrated on making oil monotypes. In 1981 I picked up the airbrush and swung into ultra-realism. Working from the flowers I grew, I sprayed canvases with acrylic images up to 5 x 8 feet. After 10 years of wearing a Niosh respirator, I had to quit spraying paint, being allergic to pigment that hung in the air. My latest work involves digital images done on the computer."

ALISON HILDRETH [1934]

FALMOUTH, MAINE

After graduating from Vassar College with a BA in Art History, Alison Hildreth worked in New York and went to night school at the Art Students League and the National Academy of Art. Afterwards she moved to Maine and continued her studies in Studio Art, graduating from the Maine College of Art in 1976. Since that time Alison has had several studios in Portland and now is located at the Bakery Studios at 61 Pine Street. Her practice includes mixed media drawing, painting, printmaking, and some installation work.

FRANCES HODSDON [1926]

JEFFERSON, MAINE

"I lived in several cities of Massachusetts, graduated from high school, and attended Swain School of Design, studying Commercial Art. I spent the next three and a half years at the Boston Museum School, majoring in Printmaking. That work culminated years later in a BFA in Printmaking at Kent State University, Kent, OH, where I did graduate work.

I have always been making prints and acquiring equipment, and have exhibited wherever I was living. I have been teaching printmaking on a part-time basis for fifty years in all media: Lithography, Etching, Silkscreen and Woodcut."

LISSA HUNTER [1945]

PORTLAND, MAINE

Lissa Hunter is a studio artist and received a BA in Fine Arts and an MFA in Textile Design from Indiana University. Her work is exhibited internationally and is in the collections of the Museum of Arts and Design in New York, the Smithsonian American Art Museum, Renwick Gallery in Washington DC, and the Museum of Fine Arts in Boston, among others, and numerous corporate and private collections. She is president of the Board of Trustees at Haystack Mountain School of Crafts, Deer Isle, ME and has enjoyed teaching and writing as part of her practice for over 30 years.

DAHLOV IPCAR [1917]
ROBINHOOD, MAINE

She was born in Windsor, VT in 1917, the daughter of artists William and Marguerite Zorach. She attended no art schools nor did her parents attempt to influence her. In 1936 she married Adoph Ipcar and moved to a farm in Maine where she has lived and painted ever since.

YVONNE JACQUETTE [1934]
SEARSMONT, MAINE & NEW YORK CITY

Yvonne Jacquette's paintings bring a sense of magic to the physical features of cityscapes and landscapes as viewed from airplanes and high buildings. Many of her works incorporate multiple perspectives or composite viewpoints while in others feathery brush-strokes abstract and soften the physical features of the landscape. Born in Pittsburgh, PA in 1934, Jacquette grew up in Stamford, CT. After attending the Rhode Island School of Design in Providence from 1952 to 1955, she moved to New York City. She continues to live and work in New York as well as in Searsmont, ME. Jacquette's work is included in the collections of over forty museums, such as the Brooklyn Museum, NY; Hirshhorn Museum and Sculpture Garden, Washington, DC; Metropolitan Museum of Art, NY; Museum of Modern Art, NY; Philadelphia Museum of Art, PA; and Whitney Museum of American Art, New York.

FRANCES KORNBLUTH [1920]
MONHEGAN, MAINE & GROSVENORDALE, CONNECTICUT

"I was born in New York City in 1920 and received a BA from Brooklyn College in 1940 as a Music Major. I was a part time student at the Brooklyn Museum School between 1951 and 1955 then earned an MAE from Pratt Institute in 1962. My mentors and teachers were Reuben Tam and Robert Richenburg. After marrying in 1940 I worked for the Lend Lease Organization and for the Office of Strategic Services in Washington, DC. I established a summer studio on Monhegan Island, Maine in 1954 and a winter studio in North Grosvenordale, Connecticut in 1969."

ROSE MARASCO [1948]
PORTLAND, MAINE

Rose Marasco is a highly accomplished artist and educator. Solo exhibitions include: the Houston Center for Photography; Université de Bretagne Occidentale, France; Sarah Morthland Gallery, NYC; the Davis Museum/Wellesley College; and, the Farnsworth Museum of Art.

Marasco's work has been published in *The New York Times, The New Yorker, New York, The Chronicle of Higher Education, The Boston Globe,* and *The Village Voice.* Her work is in numerous collections including: the Fogg Museum; Fidelity Investments Corporate Art Collection; the Davis Museum, Wellesley College; the New York Public Library; the Portland Museum of Art; and, the Museum of American History.

In 2005 she received *Excellence in Photographic Teaching Award,* from the Center, Sante Fe, NM. She is a Distinguished Professor of Art at the University of Southern Maine.

MARYLIN QUINT-ROSE [1927]
TENANTS HARBOR, MAINE

Quint-Rose has been a practicing sculptor for most of her life. Self-tutored at a young age by the collections of the Museum of Fine Art, she graduated from Wheelock College and received her MFA from the Milton Avery Graduate School of the Arts, Bard College. In the late 1960s, while teaching at the School of the Worcester Art Museum, she discovered the possibilities of working with handmade paper and since then it has become her primary medium.

Dedicated to her art and teaching, Quint-Rose has directed numerous workshops and residencies in design, collage, and papermaking for children and adults throughout New England and has been a frequent guest lecturer at the university level. She has shown internationally and is collected by several corporations and museums.

KATARINA WESLIEN [1952]
PORTLAND, MAINE

Katarina Weslien was born in Sweden and received her MFA from Cranbrook Academy of Art. She is the recipient of numerous awards including from the National Endowment for the Arts. Exhibitions include Portland Museum of Art; School of the Art Institute of Chicago; Bates Museum, Maine; Women's Museum, Washington DC; MASS MoCA. Her work is in the collection of the Metropolitan Museum of Art, Portland Museum of Art, and Cranbrook Academy of Art, among others.

She is the editor of the *Moth Press* at Maine College of Art. Currently she is Visiting Artist at the School of the Art Institute of Chicago and co-facilitates their Study Abroad program in India.

• • •

WORLDVIEW

JUDITH ALLEN-EFSTATHIOU [1945]
PORTLAND, MAINE & ATHENS, GREECE

Judith Allen-Efstathiou is a mixed media artist and graduate of the School of the Museum of Fine Arts, Boston and Tufts University. She exhibits her work in both the USA and Europe, and has been included in many international printmaking biennials throughout the world. She lives for six months of the year in Portland, Maine, and six months in Athens, Greece. She teaches drawing at the University of Southern Maine, printmaking at MECA and drawing for the University of Oregon's Study Abroad program in Athens, Greece.

KATE CHENEY CHAPPELL [1945]
KENNEBUNK, MAINE

Kate Cheney Chappell attended Chatham College and studied painting, etching and literature at the Sorbonne and L'Atelier Goetz in Paris. She is a 1983 graduate of the University of Southern Maine. A landscape painter for over 30 years, her more recent work combines printmaking techniques, mixed media collage and installation and reflects her deep concern for the natural world. Her works are in the collections of the New York Public Library, University of New England, Colby, Bates and Bowdoin Colleges, and the New Britain Museum of American Art.

MARLENE EKOLA GERBERICK [1935]
BATH, MAINE

From early childhood Marlene Ekola Gerberick was completely engulfed by the profound beauty and mysteries of northern forests and clear, deep lakes Her very soul was fed by the intensity of solitary experience. She was embraced by mysteries and wonders, first in the Lake Superior region where she was born into the Finnish immigrant culture, and then increasingly, in Finland itself where she has spent much time in personal and professional pursuits. Curious, questioning, wondering, searching for meaning have all continued to be a part of her long life as she grew up, moving from one country to the another, and to diverse sections of the US. As well, her artistic gifts have extended from painting to poetry. She has taught and lectured and exhibited from Maine to Michigan, to New York and beyond. She has been the subject of articles from *The New York Times* to Finnish national magazines. Her works are found in collections from California to Cambodia. She has been settled in Maine since 1985.

JUDY ELLIS GLICKMAN [1938]
CAPE ELIZABETH, MAINE

"Growing up in a photographic environment in Oakland, California, I spent much of my childhood either in front of my father's huge Graflex camera or in his darkroom witnessing the magical creation of black and white photographic imagery. To this day I remain in awe. My years in Maine have allowed me to find and to express myself photographically. For this I am most grateful."

REBECCA GOODALE [1953]
FREEPORT, MAINE

By working thematically for over a decade, Rebecca Goodale has developed a vocabulary of methods and innovative forms while simultaneously doing her own brand of fieldwork. In order to gain a better understanding of each plant or animal that will become a part of her next Artist's Book she wanders into the woods and marshes by herself or with local naturalists.

Most of the work is printed and bound in small limited editions by the artist in her studios in Portland and Freeport.

Her books can be found in many other institutional collections including the Maine Women Writers Collection; Bowdoin College Library; Library of Congress; Portland Museum of Art; State Art Museum of Hawai'i; and the Fogg Museum Fine Art Library, Harvard University.

BARBARA GOODBODY [1936]
CUMBERLAND FORESIDE, MAINE

"As a young teenager *Life* and *National Geographic* were my favorite magazines. They brought the world to my finger tips! Later, with my three children "out of the nest" and a desire to explore a new path, I gave myself a 50th birthday present at the Maine Photographic Workshops in Rockport, Maine (now the Maine Media Workshops + College). Ernst Haas, a Magnum, *Life* photographer and instructor at the Workshops presented his work that first week and I was hooked! Twenty-six years later, my work has been published and shown at the United Nations, in museums, galleries, high schools and universities in the USA and at UNESCO in Paris, France. And I have had a wonderful time!"

NATASHA MAYERS [1946]
WHITEFIELD, MAINE

Natasha Mayers: artist, educator, activist. "Natasha Mayers is arguably the state's most prolific and respected activist artist. For decades, she has blurred the lines between visual art and activism, guided by an informed and conscience-driven sense of ethics while deeply concerned with the experience and virtues of civic engagement and public life." (Nicholas Schroeder in *Maine Art New.*)

Mayers has supervised more than 600 murals as a touring artist since 1975. She has taught students from nursery school to college and in diverse populations: immigrants, refugees, prisoners, the homeless, and the "psychiatrically labeled." In her own painting, Mayers often explores themes of peace and social justice. In her *State of War* series, by placing images of war onto Maine's landscape, she asks, "How would we feel if it happened here?" An empathetic response requires imagination.

ARLA PATCH [1950]
SOUTH PARIS, MAINE

Arla Patch, BFA, Ed., MFA, studied at Tyler School of Art in Philadelphia, PA and Rome, Italy, and did her graduate work at Indiana University, Bloomington, IN. She has exhibited and taught both in the US and abroad and has published two award-winning books: *A Body Story* and *Finding Ground: Girls and Women in Recovery*.

Within a 40-year career teaching and leading workshops, the last 20 years have had a focus on using art for recovery from trauma. She has used art as a tool for healing personally and with women in prison, at risk teens, those recovering from cancer and sexual abuse.

ABBY SHAHN [1940]
SOLON, MAINE

"I was born into a family of visual artists. I grew up in central New Jersey. When I was young, I rebelled. I was going to be a poet. Poems spilled out of my mind onto paper. Then I went to college and began to paint. I quickly got hooked. I quit college and went to San Francisco and then on to NYC. I've been painting ever since then. In the early sixties we bought an old farm in Maine and started coming here in the summers. In the late sixties, urban renewal took our loft away. We had two small children. We decided to try a winter up in Maine. I've lived here ever since then, and I enjoy it more and more."

ALICE SPENCER [1944]
PORTLAND, MAINE

Alice Spencer has lived and worked in Maine for over 40 years. She is a printmaker as well as a painter and is co-founder of the Peregrine Press, a printmaking cooperative in Portland. She has taught printmaking at Maine College of Art's continuing studies, Haystack School of Crafts, and in Mongolia and Zanzibar, Tanzania. She helped organize print exchanges between her students abroad and Maine printmakers. She chaired the city of Portland's Public Art Committee for 15 years and in 2009 received the Maine College of Art's award for Leadership in the Arts. Spencer has had numerous one-person exhibits. Her work has been shown throughout Maine, New England, Canada and at US embassies in Chile and Sarajevo, Herzegovina. She is represented by Aucocisco Galleries.

MELITA WESTERLUND [1945]
BAR HARBOR, MAINE

Melita Westerlund was born in Helsinki, Finland and studied art in Finland, Tunis, and the USA. She received her undergraduate degree from the University of Industrial Arts, Helsinki and MFA from SUNY, Buffalo. She is currently on the Adjunct Faculty of the College of the Atlantic. Westerlund is a member of the Sculpture Society of Finland and the International Sculpture Society. She has exhibited widely throughout New England with recent solo exhibitions in Helsinki, Finland. Her work is found in more than 20 private collections and she has received several Percent for Art awards from the Maine Arts Commission.

• • •

DIRIGO

SUSAN AMONS [1954]
BIDDEFORD, MAINE

Susan Amons has been a working artist in Maine for 35 years. She received her BFA in Painting from Massachusetts College of Art in 1976. Susan has completed 14 printmaking Fellowships at the Womens' Studio Workshop, Rosendale, NY, and six Fellowships at the Vermont Studio Center. She is a member of the Peregrine Press, and the National Association of Women Artists, whose illustrious members have included Mary Cassatt, Judy Chicago, and Audrey Flack.

Susan Amons is represented by numerous galleries in Maine and New York. Her work is included in the collections of the Portland Museum of Art, the Farnsworth Museum, University of New England, Colby, Bates, and Bowdoin College collections, the Boston, and New York Public Libraries, and the Zimmerli Museum, Rutgers University, New Jersey.

KELIY ANDERSON-STALEY [1977]
GUILFORD, MAINE & RUSSELLVILLE, ARKANSAS

Keliy Anderson-Staley was raised "off the grid" in Maine, earned a BA from Hampshire College in Massachusetts and an MFA from Hunter College in New York. She has been awarded a Howard Foundation Fellowship, New York Foundation for the Arts Fellowship and a Puffin Grant. Solo exhibitions of her work were mounted at Light Work in Syracuse, Palitz Gallery in NYC, Southeast Museum of Photography, California Museum of Photography and John Cleary Gallery in Houston. Her work has been included in shows at the Portland Museum of Art, Catherine Edelman Gallery and a number of other galleries nationally and internationally. Her work is in the collections of the Library of Congress, the Portland Museum of Art, the Southeast Museum of Photography, Cedar Rapids Museum of Art and Bidwell Projects.

JOSEFINA AUSLENDER [1934]
CAPE ELIZABETH, MAINE

An Argentine, she was educated in visual arts at the Perugino School and the Escuela Nacional de Bellas Artes Prilidiano Puryrredon of Buenos Aires, where she finished with the degree of professor in Visual Arts. In 1968 she was awarded Third Prize in the Salon Nacional de Ceramica. In 1973 she won First Mention, Salon Manuel Belgrano de dibujo (drawing) in the Museo Sivori. In 1975 she won Third Prize at the Bienal Santa Maria del Buen Aire in the Museo de Arte Moderno. She was awarded Premio Bull in the Fifth Bienal de Madonado, Uruguay in 1985. In 1988 she moved to Maine where she works and shows periodically.

DOZIER BELL [1957]
WALDOBORO, MAINE

Dozier Bell is a Maine native whose work has been featured in over thirty solo shows in New York City and across the country. She is the recipient of a number of national awards, including a National Endowment for the Arts Fellowship, a Fulbright Fellowship, two Pollock-Krasner Foundation Grants, and the Adolf and Esther Gottlieb Foundation Grant. She is represented by the Danese Gallery in New York City and Aucocisco Galleries in Portland, Maine.

MELONIE BENNETT [1969]
GORHAM, MAINE

"I grew up on a dairy farm in Gorham, Maine and graduated from the Maine College of Art with a BFA in Photography in 1991. I have worked with photographer, Judy Ellis Glickman, since graduating college. I have had the opportunity to photograph assignments for Down East Magazine and have received an Aaron Siskind Foundation Individual Photographer Fellowship as well as a Maine Arts Commission Individual Artist Fellowship."

KATHERINE BRADFORD [1942]

BRUNSWICK, MAINE & BROOKLYN, NEW YORK

Katherine Bradford began her life as a painter in Brunswick, Maine and now splits her time between Maine and New York. She is represented by Aucocisco Galleries in Portland and Edward Thorp Gallery in New York City. In 2009 she was a resident faculty at Skowhegan and in 2011 she was awarded a Guggenheim Fellowship. This year she had a one person exhibit in New York and was included in CMCA[1]s 60th Anniversary exhibition honoring five artists for their contributions to contemporary art in Maine. Her most recent show at Edward Thorp Gallery was favorably reviewed in The New York Times (5/03/12).

ALLISON COOKE BROWN [1950]

YARMOUTH, MAINE

Allison Cooke Brown's art centers on her own personal experiences. She was raised in a traditional Calvinist New England family consisting of mostly women, and was taught at an early age how to sew. This sensibility runs throughout most of her art and explains an inclination to use "women's work" as her language to discuss gender issues.

KATHERINE COBEY [1938]

CUSHING, MAINE

Katharine Cobey's works have been exhibited in museums across the country. Voyageur Press calls her the "founder of sculptural knitting." In 2010, her book *Diagonal Knitting* was published by Schoolhouse Press and hailed by *Vogue Knitting* as a classic; and she was named a Maine Master Craft Artist by the Maine Crafts Association.

GRACE DeGENNARO [1956]

YARMOUTH, MAINE

Grace DeGennaro received an MFA from Columbia University and a BS from Skidmore College. Working in the tradition of geometric abstraction, her oil paintings and watercolors utilize traditional symbols and a nonlinear perspective. She is the recipient of grants from the Ballinglen Arts Foundation, the New England Foundation for the Arts, and the Maine Arts Commission. Her work has been exhibited widely including at the Heckscher Museum of Art, Huntington, NY, the Portland Museum of Art, Portland, ME, The Painting Center, New York, NY, The Visual Arts Center of New Jersey, Summit, NJ and the Kentler International Drawing Space, Brooklyn, NY. She is represented by Aucocisco Galleries.

DENISE FROEHLICH [1967]

PORTLAND, MAINE

Denise Froehlich has been a fine art photographer for more than 20 years and her work is often autobiographical in nature. Denise's photographs can be found in New England museums and academic institutions as well as in many private collections throughout the country. She is also a professor of art and has taught at numerous academic institutions including Bates College, College of the Atlantic, University of New England and New England School of Art and Design/Suffolk. Recently she co-launched with Elizabeth Moss, Anne B. Zill and Melonie Bennett, the Maine Museum of Photographic Arts where she is the director of education.

MEGGAN GOULD [1976]

HARPSWELL, MAINE

Meggan Gould is a photographer living and working in Brunswick, Maine, where she has taught photography at Bowdoin College since 2006. She studied photography at Speos, Paris Photographic Institute, and the University of Massachusetts at Dartmouth, where she received her Masters of Fine Arts. Gould has exhibited widely in the United States and internationally. She is primarily interested in using photography to examine how photographs shape our vision.

MARY HART [1960]

PORTLAND, MAINE

Mary Hart was born in 1960 in Woodbury, CT. Her childhood was shaped by her mother's training in the natural sciences and by many hours spent observing, collecting and identifying natural specimens. Hart's mature work is known for its close observation of natural forms. She currently lives, paints and teaches in southern Maine. She is represented by Aucocisco Galleries.

JANICE KASPAR [1950]

SWANVILLE, MAINE

Janice Kasper has lived year-round in the Belfast area since 1974. She received a BFA in painting from the University of Connecticut in 1973 and was a scholarship student at the Skowhegan School of Painting & Sculpture in 1979. The focus of her artistic and private life is the protection of wildlife and wild lands. She was awarded artist-in-residence positions at Denali National Park in Alaska in 2007 and Isle Royale National Park in Michigan in 2009.

Her work can be found in the collection of the Portland Museum of Art, the Farnsworth Art Museum and the University of Maine. She is represented by Caldbeck Gallery in Rockland, Maine.

ELIZABETH CASHIN MCMILLEN [1940]

MARLBORO, MAINE

Elizabeth Cashin McMillen was born in Chicago, Illinois. The family spent summers at their farm in Michigan which provided the model for her home in Maine where she has lived since the 1970s. Art was prominent in her home and education. The years her family lived in Mexico broadened her interest to include ancient architectural sites and artifacts, to the *churrigueresque* cathedrals and vivid culture of folk art.

Art became and would remain a lens for translation. She is represented by Aucocisco Galleries.

CELESTE ROBERGE [1951]

SOUTH PORTLAND, MAINE & GAINESVILLE, FLORIDA

Celeste Roberge was born in Biddeford, Maine. She resides in Maine and in Florida where she is Professor of Sculpture at the School of Art + Art History, University of Florida. She received a BFA from the Maine College of Art, MFA from Nova Scotia College of Art & Design, and attended the Skowhegan School of Painting and Sculpture.

NORIKO SAKANISHI [1939]

PORTLAND, MAINE

"I came to the United States from Japan to study at Westbrook College (now UNE). At Westbrook, I discovered art and went on to attend the Portland School of Art (now MECA). I majored in sculpture and began my professional career carving wood and stone. Unfortunately, I developed a severe shoulder problem and had to give up carving or risk further injury. I continued to think as a sculptor, however, and gradually invented a way of working in three-dimensions with lighter materials as well as adding color to my work."

BARBARA SULLIVAN [1950]

SOLON, MAINE

Barbara Sullivan works in true buon fresco. Her work celebrates and satirizes our daily quotidian. She teaches at the University of Maine at Farmington. She holds a BA in Art and Creative Writing from UMF, and an MFA from Vermont College. She has twice received the Adolph and Esther Gottlieb Foundation Grant, a Pollock/Krasner Grant, and a Maine Arts Commission Good Idea Grant. In 1999 she completed a Percent for Art Project for the Cross Office Building at the State House in Augusta. Sullivan has been included three times in the Portland Museum of Art Biennial. She has shown widely in Maine and beyond.

DIANE BOWIE ZAITLIN [1950]

SACO, MAINE

Diane Bowie Zaitlin has lived most of her life on the coast of Maine. Although this is not literally evident in her artwork, it is reflected in the feeling of ebb and flow, birth and rebirth, and observation of patterns and color in nature. Working as an artist in Maine creates a rhythmic response and wonder at both the stark, quiet lack of color and the energetic exuberance of color.

• • •

Alicia Eggert, *Equation: art = people + place x time*

CHECKLIST